WRITERS AND AUTHORS

PRACTICAL CAREER GUIDES

Series Editor: Kezia Endsley

Clean Energy Technicians, by Marcia Santore
Computer Game Development & Animation, by Tracy Brown Hamilton
Craft Artists, by Marcia Santore
Criminal Justice Professionals, by Kezia Endsley
Culinary Arts, by Tracy Brown Hamilton
Dental Assistants and Hygienists, by Kezia Endsley
Education Professionals, by Kezia Endsley
Electricians, by Marcia Santore
Fine Artists, by Marcia Santore
First Responders, by Kezia Endsley
Health and Fitness Professionals, by Kezia Endsley
Information Technology (IT) Professionals, by Erik Dafforn
Mathematicians and Statisticians, by Kezia Endsley
Media and Journalism Professionals, by Tracy Brown Hamilton
Medical Office Professionals, by Marcia Santore
Multimedia and Graphic Designers, by Kezia Endsley
Nursing Professionals, by Kezia Endsley
Plumbers, by Marcia Santore
Skilled Trade Professionals, by Corbin Collins
Veterinarian Technicians and Assistants, by Kezia Endsley
Writers and Authors, by Tracy Brown Hamilton

WRITERS AND AUTHORS
A Practical Career Guide

TRACY BROWN HAMILTON

ROWMAN & LITTLEFIELD
Lanham • Boulder • New York • London

Published by Rowman & Littlefield
An imprint of The Rowman & Littlefield Publishing Group, Inc.
4501 Forbes Boulevard, Suite 200, Lanham, Maryland 20706
www.rowman.com

6 Tinworth Street, London SE11 5AL, United Kingdom

British Library Cataloguing in Publication Information Available

Library of Congress Cataloging-in-Publication Data

Names: Hamilton, Tracy Brown, author.
Title: Writers and authors : a practical career guide / Tracy Brown Hamilton.
Description: Lanham : Rowman & Littlefield, [2021] | Series: Practical career guides | Includes bibliographical references. | Summary: "Writers and Authors: A Practical Career Guide, which includes interviews with professionals in the field, covers the following areas of this field that have proven to be stable, lucrative, and growing professions in the following fields, biographers, bloggers, content writers, copywriters, novelists, playwrights, screenwriters, and speechwriters"—Provided by publisher.
Identifiers: LCCN 2021003804 (print) | LCCN 2021003805 (ebook) | ISBN 9781538144817 (paperback) | ISBN 9781538144824 (epub)
Subjects: LCSH: Authorship—Vocational guidance.
Classification: LCC PN151 .H326 2021 (print) | LCC PN151 (ebook) | DDC 808.02023—dc23
LC record available at https://lccn.loc.gov/2021003804
LC ebook record available at https://lccn.loc.gov/2021003805

Contents

Introduction

Welcome to a Career as a Writer!

That you picked this book off the shelf and are reading it indicates that you are ready to take your curiosity, writing skills, and talent for storytelling to the next level by considering writing as a career.

Unlike other fields with more concrete career paths, the road to becoming a writer or an author can feel less straightforward—with fewer guarantees. There are many different paths—both in terms of education and life experience—that can lead you to publishing your writing and many different types of job options that will enable you to apply your writing and researching skills to inform and entertain your audience.

It may seem confusing to separate an author from a writer, but in the simplest terms, all authors are writers but not all writers are authors. Merriam-Webster defines an author as "the writer of a literary work (such as a book)" whereas a writer is defined as "one who writes" (such as the writer of an article, blog, or advertising copy).[1]

This book will primarily focus on the path to becoming a creative writer—meaning an author of fiction, short fiction, or poetry, but because many aspiring writers and authors rely on (and often enjoy) a day job to provide steady income, this book will also discuss paths to finding professional writing jobs such as technical writer, copywriter, or blogger as well as non-writing jobs that require a background in literature and publishing such as editor or literary agent.

Being a professional writer requires superior writing skills, naturally, but also research skills and a talent for selecting subject matter that will resonate with your editors and audience. The life of a writer typically involves

- identifying subjects that will interest and attract an audience
- writing fiction or nonfiction scripts, biographies, poems, or works in other genres and formats

- researching heavily to inform and support work in various subject matters
- working closely with editors to polish and shape content for publication or broadcasting

This book is the ideal start for understanding the various careers available to you within the writing industry, which one will be right for you, and what path you should follow to ensure you have all the training, education, and experience needed to succeed in your future career goals. It also includes advice on how to make contacts, identify stories, and pitch ideas.

Whether you have the ambition to write novels, poems, short stories, film scripts, or a blog or memoir, this book will help you understand how to begin now, whether you are a high school student or a university graduate, to set yourself on the course to a successful career as a writer or author.

A Career as a Writer or Author

Writers and authors play a very important role in society. Writers apply their command of language to research, produce, and edit anything from novels to poems, articles to creative nonfiction. As mentioned, many aspiring creative writers also hold a day job as a writing instructor, editor, professor, or business writer while simultaneously working on their own, personal writing. And a vast majority of writers work as freelancers, which also requires a strong network, a loyal audience, and savviness in pitching your work and seeking out new clients.

Here are some jobs available for creative writers.

- *Biographer*—Conduct research into a person's life and write an informative, accurate, engaging account of it
- *Blogger*—Write posts on a particular subject—from sports to literature to parenting to health. Bloggers can work professionally for a company or organization or build their own audience as an individual.
- *Content writer*—Write about any topic of interest unlike writers who usually specialize in a given field
- *Copywriter*—Write content for companies or advertising agencies, producing advertising slogans and other content

- ***Novelist***—Write books of fiction, creating characters and plots that may be imaginary or based on real events
- ***Playwright***—Write scripts for the theater, including writing the dialog and stage directions
- ***Screenwriter***—Write scripts for movies and television
- ***Speechwriter***—Write speeches for business leaders, politicians, and others who engage in public speaking in their careers

The Market Today

How does the job market look for young people seeking to work as writers or authors? The outlook is slightly mixed. On one hand, people will always want to read for information and for the entertainment produced by talented creative writers. And technology and other changes in business practices—self-publishing, blogging, online publishing to name a few—have enabled more writers to access an audience without having to sign with a mainstream publisher. At the same time, this has made it harder to gain attention because there are so many other writers vying for the same audience. Social networking such as Twitter and Instagram have given writers platforms to build a solid following and gain the attention of major publishers and other media outlets, but it's a crowded space and a very competitive one.

> "You can have a rich editing or teaching career and a fulfilling life as a creative writer at the same time, and one can support the other, but you need to be intentional about it."—Nicole VanderLinden, freelance editor, journal reviewer, and author of short fiction

At the same time, according to the U.S. Bureau of Labor Statistics (BLS), jobs for writers and authors will decline by just over 2 percent from 2019 to 2029.[2] In 2019, according to the BLS, there were 131,200 jobs for writers and authors in the United States and this is predicted to drop by 3,100 by 2029.

Figure i.1. Becoming a professional writer or editor is an ambitious goal, but that should not discourage you. Hard work and dedication to honing your skills will help you find an outlet through which to share your story. *1001Love/iStock/Getty Images.*

What Does This Book Cover?

This book covers the following topics as well as others.

- understanding what writers and authors do and what characteristics many who land in these fields possess
- forming a career plan—starting now, wherever you are in your education—and taking the steps that will best lead to success
- learning your educational requirements and opportunities and how to fulfill them
- knowing how to write your résumé, interview, network, and apply for jobs
- finding additional resources for further information

Where Do You Start?

No matter where you are in your education, from junior high to college graduate or beyond, it is never too soon to get started pursuing a career in any field of writing. The more you write, the better you will become—and that will remain true throughout your career. Believe in your work but not so much that there isn't room for improvement. Any type of writing you do, from a social media post to a novel, will help you develop your ability and find your voice.

Also, it is essential that you read. You are very unlikely to succeed as a writer if you do not have an appreciation of, if not an addiction to, the work of others. Being able to critique and analyze what you read—knowing why a piece of writing works for you or why it doesn't—can teach you a lot about improving your own writing.

> "I kept always two books in my pocket, one to read, one to write in."—Robert Louis Stevenson (1850–1894), Scottish novelist, poet, and travel writer

Once you've read this book, you will be well on your way to understanding what kind of career path you want, what you can expect from it, and how to go about planning and beginning that path. Let's get started!

1

Why Choose a Career in Writing?

*T*here are many reasons people decide to become a writer or author—or in many cases, become a writer or author without it having been their original career goal at all. Many writers follow completely different educational paths and, along the way, discover a story they want to tell. Others have the ambition to become a writer early on, focusing on writing and literature courses or, if not interested in pursuing a college degree, honing their craft on their own or taking various writing workshops and other courses to sharpen their skills.

Unlike more conventional, straightforward career paths, there are many routes one can take to become a writer or an author. What they all have in common is, ultimately, the desire to write and the ability to do so, which entails certain characteristics: not only a strong sense of language but an enduring curiosity about people and the world, the ability to observe and listen and see the stories that surround us every day then be able to tell those stories in an engaging way with words.

A future as a writer or author offers you an opportunity to be continuously learning, whether you are working as a novelist, a writing instructor, a journalist, or a business writer. It will help you become a more coherent thinker, demanding that you consider deeply what you think and what you want to say about a particular subject—whether you are working on a blog post, a poem, a play, or a novel. The ability to express yourself articulately and find just the right word, just the right expression to convey what you mean, is an incredibly valuable skill to develop, both in your profession and your life.

"Don't bend; don't water it down; don't try to make it logical; don't edit your own soul according to the fashion. Rather, follow your most intense obsessions mercilessly."— Franz Kafka (1883–1924), German-Jewish novelist and short-fiction writer

---

Becoming a writer or author is a very competitive goal, which will be discussed later in the book, so pursuing either takes a thick skin (there will be a lot of rejection and constructive criticism), perseverance, and a strong belief in your project so you don't give up. As with all pursuits, there is no guarantee of success. But you can't let that discourage you.

Choosing a career is a difficult task, but as we discuss in more detail in chapter 2, there are many methods and means of support to help you refine your career goal and hone in on a path to achieving it that will fit you the best. This chapter will define the writing profession as well as look at the predicted future of the field.

What Do Writers and Authors Do?

The most obvious answer to what writers and authors do is they write—in different styles, and for different audiences and purposes, but the core function of a writer or author is to convey information and tell stories with written words. But of course it goes deeper than that. Writers and authors have a strong command of language, a strong ability to come up with ideas, and the research skills to see a project through authentically.

The information provided in this book is focused primarily on creative writing—which is the writing done by playwrights, novelists, authors of short fiction, memoirists, and poets, for example. But many aspiring and professional, published creative writers also have (and often enjoy) a day job to ensure a steady income while they pursue and complete creative projects—a job such as blogger, journalist, copy writer, technical writer, or editor or literary agent. The information provided here will also be relevant to these pursuits.

"The best writing, I think, comes from what we want or need to write, from the desire to engage in the writing process, and from trusting your instincts to follow certain ideas. Keeping journals of ideas and notes has helped me to trust in my ideas and in my process of developing them."—George Guida, author, poet, and professor of literature and creative writing

The following briefly describes several careers in creative writing and publishing.

FICTION AUTHOR

Authors of fiction write original works in narrative form that are based on imagined people, places, and events. A manuscript of over 40,000 words is considered a *novel*; a manuscript between 7,500 and 39,000 words is considered a *novella*; and anything under 7,500 words is considered a *short story*.

CREATIVE NONFICTION AUTHOR

Authors of creative nonfiction write factual essays or memoirs using the same literary approaches and techniques as fiction writers. Neil Gutkind, founder of the online magazine *Creative Nonfiction*, defines creative nonfiction as "true stories, well told."[1]

POET

Poetry is a form a literature that differs from prose in its structure. It is structured in lines rather than paragraphs and is heavily reliant on rhythm and meter. A poet, naturally, is one who writes poems.

Note: While many bloggers are also creative nonfiction writers, blogging itself is not a form of writing but a platform. Many published authors began growing an audience by blogging, and it is a good way to indicated to a potential editor or literary agent that your book idea has strong potential in the marketplace. Blogging also gives you the opportunity to practice writing and developing your voice, which will be a key to your success.

EDITOR

An editor is someone who works either as a freelancer or with a media or publishing house to guide a writer or author in polishing and refining a written work to prepare it for a publication. There are many types of editors: *acquisitions editors* who sign authors and prepare contracts; *development editors* who work with the author on the overall structure and execution of the work; and *copyeditors* who focus on detailed aspects such as grammar and punctuation.

LITERARY AGENT

The role of the literary agent is to represent an author and help him or her sell their work. This entails packaging a proposal and submitting it to various editors, and this in turn requires knowledge of the publishing market and current trends. Agents also work as a liaison between authors and publishers to finalize contracts.

Figure 1.1. There are many paths to becoming a writer or an author but all require similar sets of skills, including writing and researching prowess, as well as personal characteristics such as drive and persistence. *jakkapan21/iStock/Getty Images.*

A CASE FOR AND AGAINST WRITING FOR FREE TO GAIN EXPERIENCE

One challenge aspiring and even working writers and authors face is how they feel about being asked to write for no money. This can be seen as both an opportunity for exposure to an audience and as a way to build a portfolio of your published work, but it can also be seen as exploitative. You would never, for example, be expected to do someone's accounting for free just to build your reputation as an accountant. But being an accountant is different from being a writer (or an aspiring one) so the debate of whether you should write for free is a somewhat murky one.

Writing for free can mean publishing your own blog for your own reasons, whether you want to share personal stories of travel or grief or animal care or whatever subject it is that you wish to focus on in your blog. Many authors have earned book deals because of the platform they built via writing a personal blog for free. Writer Nick Douglas suggests on www.lifehacker.com that anyone wishing to become a professional writer not only should but needs to write for free as a means of achieving that goal—not only because it can gain you an audience but because it gives you the artistic freedom to grow and develop your own voice and style and improve your writing overall.

> You can get artistic, or you can concentrate on a marketable idea. It'd be wise to choose something you actually care about, rather than chase money, but I won't pretend the latter never got anyone a book deal and a spot at Urban Outfitters. But consider all the formats available—a group blog, a podcast, YouTube sketches, a basement theater company.[2]

But often writers are asked to write for businesses for free, and author and blogger John Scalzi makes a strong argument against doing so.

> My definition of "writing for free" is writing work that is *aimed at the stream of commerce* but for which one is not compensated for its production. More simply, work where *someone* is trying to make money off it, but none of that money gets to *me*. By that definition, no personal blog post, tweet, Facebook posting, email, etc. constitutes "free" writing, since none of it was ever intended in itself to make money. But things I write for others are almost always in the stream of commerce—and somewhere along the way, someone is getting paid because of it, or at least trying to.[3]

Many writers argue that the danger and negative effect of writing for no financial compensation for publications that are earning revenue from your work brings down the overall rates writers can be expected to earn for their work, so while it might get you some bylines, it can also have a lasting impact on the living you can make as a writer. But it's a choice to make for yourself.

The Pros and Cons of Becoming a Writer or Author

As with any career, being a writer or author has upsides and downsides. But it is also true that one person's pro is another person's con. Although it's impossible to describe a career as a writer or author definitively, there are some generalizations that can be made when it comes to what is most challenging or most gratifying about the work.

> "I hate writing. I love having written."—Dorothy Parker (1893–1967), American poet, writer, and critic

Here are some general pros.

- You get to do what you love and apply your writing, researching, and editing skills—and continuously develop them—to subjects you feel passionate about.
- Your work will be incredibly creative and challenging and never routine. Most every day, every story, every project will be different from the next.
- You will have colleagues or other professional contacts, such as editors and literary agents, who share, believe in, and support your ideas and from whom you can learn.
- You'll find a vast degree of variety in work environments, from large corporations to startups to freelance work anywhere in the world.
- You can make a real difference by shedding light on issues or people or stories that you are passionate about.

And here are some general cons.

- It can take a long time to be published, and the process can be grueling and discouraging.
- Very few authors are able to rely solely on their earnings from their creative work and work a day job for financial security, so the hours can be long. And as far as salaries and growth in media and journalism go, the predictions show future declines.

- Succeeding as a freelance writer, whether you're trying to sell an article or a novel, requires a lot of self-promotion to build an audience and attract the attention of editors and agents. Networking, creating a strong social media presence, and having the ability to accept rejection are all part of the job.
- You'll often spend a lot of time—a lot—conceptualizing, researching, and writing with no guarantee that your work will see publication. You have to believe enough in your own idea to accept that it may take a while for an editor or agent to share your vision.

How Healthy Is the Job Market for Writers and Authors?

In the world of writers and authors, salaries vary so much that it is nearly impossible to predict what your income might be. The following are general predictions of the U.S. Bureau of Labor Statistics (BLS), but keep in mind they are broad and not specific to creative literary careers.

WRITER OR AUTHOR

- Hourly pay: $30.39
- Annual wage: $63,200
- Projected growth (2019–2029)—2 percent decline

LITERARY AGENT[4]

- Hourly pay (median): $35.45
- Annual wage: $63,200
- Projected growth (2019–2029)—2 percent decline

EDITOR[5]

- Hourly pay: $29.50
- Annual pay: $61,370
- Projected growth (2019–2029)—7 percent decline

While some authors make millions, others find additional income through freelance or full-time work. This was not always the case. "In the twentieth century, a good literary writer could earn a middle-class living just writing," Mary Rasenberger, executive director of the Authors Guild, states,[6] citing Amazon's large share of self-publishing, e-book, and resale markets. Another reason it's become harder to earn a living purely from being a writer or an author is a decline in sales. According to the American Association of Publishers, sales of adult fiction fell 16 percent between 2013 and 2017, from $5.21 billion to $4.38 billion.[7] Fiction sales, rather than nonfiction sales, have been hit harder because it is more difficult to give exposure to a new fiction writer. Before online bookselling became the norm and many brick-and-mortar stores closed their doors, publishers could rely on readers to browse the shelves and discover new books. That is less and less the case now.

In contrast to this discouraging news, this seems to be turning around. Despite the closure of major chain bookstores, the number of independent bookstores rose by 35 percent between 2009 and 2015.[8] Although it is a fluctuating market, people will always want to read and to discover new writers and new ideas so there's no need to be overly discouraged by these statistics.

No matter what you are writing, the task can be just as frustrating as it is fulfilling. But keep going. *RichVintage/E+/Getty Images.*

WHAT IS A MEDIAN INCOME?

Throughout your job search, you might hear the term *median income* used. What does it mean? Some people believe it's the same thing as *average income*, but that's not correct. While median income and average income might sometimes be similar, they are calculated in different ways.

The true definition of median income is the income at which half of the workers earn more than that income and the other half of workers earn less. If this seems complicated, think of it this way: Suppose there are five employees in a company, each with varying skills and experience. Here are their salaries.

- $42,500
- $48,250
- $51,600
- $63,120
- $86,325

What is the median income? In this case, the median income is $51,600 because of the five salaries listed, it is the one in the middle. Two salaries are higher than $51,600, and two are lower.

The average income, on the other hand, is simply the total of all these salaries, divided by the number of salaries. In this case, the average income is $58,359 (291,795/5 = 58,359).

Why does this matter? Median income is a more accurate way to measure the various incomes in a set because it's less likely to be influenced by extremely high or low numbers in the total group of salaries. For example, in our example of five incomes, the highest income ($86,325) is much higher than the other incomes and therefore it makes the average income ($58,359) well higher than most incomes in the group. Therefore, if you base your income expectations on the average, you'll likely be disappointed to eventually learn that most incomes are below it.

But if you look at median income, you'll always know that half your peers are above it and half are below it. That way, depending on your level of experience and training, you'll have a better estimate of where you are on the salary spectrum.

Note: In 2008 the BLS reported that the number of people registered as self-employed writers and authors was 83,968.[9] And according to www.fastcompany.com,[10] as of October 2019 approximately 35 percent of the American workforce were freelancers in fields including and other than writing.

HIGHEST INCOME-EARNING AUTHORS

Although it is ill-advised to expect you will become a million-dollar author overnight, some writers of course do achieve this level of success. Be advised, though, that writing as a means of "chasing money" rather than writing as a means of expressing your creativity and writing stories you believe need telling is unlikely to succeed.

Below are some of the highest-paid writers based on 2018 statistics as compiled by www.selfpublishing.com.[11]

1. James Patterson, $86 million—A popular writer of thriller novels, Patterson has also coauthored a novel with former U.S. president Bill Clinton.
2. J. K. Rowling, $54 million—Rowling is internationally known as the author of the enormously popular Harry Potter series, the most successful children's book series of all time.
3. Stephen King, $27 million—King is famous for his horror fiction, and many of his books have been adapted to film. His career has spanned decades.
4. John Grisham, $21 million—Lawyer-turned-author of legal thrillers, Grisham has authored several books in this genre, including *The Firm*. Like King, many of his books have been adapted to film.
5. Jeff Kinney, $18.5 million—Kinney is the author of the children's novel *Diary of a Wimpy Kid*.
6. Dan Brown, $13 million—Brown is the author of *The Da Vinci Code* and other novels.
7. Michael Wolff, $13 million—The only nonfiction writer on this list, Wolff is the author of *Fire and Fury*, which examines the inner-workings of the Donald Trump administration.
8. Danielle Steel, $12 million—Steel is the author of many romance novels.
9. Nora Roberts, $12 million—Roberts is another best-selling romance novelist.
10. Rick Riordan, $10.5 million—Riordan is the author of the Percy Jackson series.

Am I Right for a Career as a Writer or Author?

This is a tough question to answer because really the answer can only come from you. But don't despair. There are plenty of resources both online and elsewhere that can help you find the answer by guiding you through the types of questions and considerations that will bring you to your conclusion. These are covered in more detail in chapter 2. But for now, let's look at the general demands and responsibilities of a career as a writer and author and suggest some questions that may help you discover whether this profession will be a good match for your personality, interests, and the general lifestyle you want to keep in the future.

> **Note:** Of course no job is going to match your personality or fit your every desire, especially when you are just starting out. There are, however, some aspects to a job that may be so unappealing or simply wrong that you may decide to opt for something else, or equally you may be so drawn to one feature of a job that any of the downsides will not be that important.

Obviously having an ability and a passion for writing, for performing research and asking questions, for reading and storytelling, and for continuously remaining curious about people in the world around you is key to success in this field—whether you are writing fiction, a memoir, or creating content for a business or magazine. But there are other factors to keep in mind. One way to see if you may be cut out for a career as an author or writer is to ask yourself the following questions.

Am I satisfied spending a lot of time in front of a computer, often in isolation, or would I prefer a more bustling work environment with many colleagues working as part of a larger team?

Again, with writing and authoring many different functions and work environments are possible. Screenwriters, for example, often work in collaboration with other writers, and of course if you are writing or editing in a professional office environment, that will also afford you colleagues and collaboration. But the image many of us have of a creative writer is someone pounding away at a keyboard in a quiet environment, and unless you have secured an agent or an editor and find yourself working on a deadline, it can be hard to find the discipline and endurance needed to keep going on your own.

Do I handle critiques well or does the idea of criticism horrify me? Can I handle rejection?

Writing is an objective business, and although your work will of course be very personal to you, unless you self-publish you will be met with criticism (although for the most part constructive!) and of course, given the competitive nature of the publishing business, there will be more nos than yeses. Rejection is part of the game. Many editors may not be interested in your work, but you have to keep going until you find one that is. This demands being open to the feedback your work receives and using it to your advantage to achieve your publication goal.

Am I a highly creative, analytical thinker who comes up with lots of ideas? Am I equally able to let an idea go or adjust it?

Similar to the point above, in most cases as a writer or an author you will not have full creative authority over what you want to write. It can be very painful to write what you believe to be the perfect passage or scene only to have an editor suggest you cut it. That is why it's very important to have a relationship with an editor you trust and believe wants to preserve your vision for your project and is working in your interest to make it as good and successful as possible. You have to be able to let go, in other words, and trust in the process.

Am I genuinely interested in other people, other points of view, and listening to and telling these stories in my writing?

Even if you are working on a memoir, it's key that you have an understanding of how your story fits into a broader context and why others will identify with and be interested in it. That takes a level of understanding of others equal to the ability of the writer of fiction to create characters and experiences that others can relate to.

Am I comfortable self-promoting, becoming in a sense my own brand? Am I willing to put time into blogging, sharing stories on social media, doing readings, teaching courses, appearing in panels at literary conferences and so on to promote my work and build my audience?

Although many publishers have public relations departments, the brunt of promoting yourself and your book will fall on your shoulders. Getting published is just the first step to being successful as a writer, and growing an audience will increase the chances that you will be able to sell your next project.

Can I work to deadline and function under pressure?

Whatever type of writing you do, deadlines can be both a blessing and curse, but they are always a reality. Some people thrive under the pressure of a tight deadline while for others they are intimidating if not terrifying.

> "Get it down. Take chances. It may be bad, but it's the only way you can do anything really good."—William Faulkner (1919–1962), American novelist, short-story writer, poet, and playwright

CULTIVATING A VOICE AND AN AUDIENCE AS A BLOGGER

Sheila Quirke.
Courtesy of Sheila Quirke.

Sheila Quirke is a freelance writer and blogger living in Chicago with her husband and two sons. Trained and experienced as a clinical social worker, she shifted gears after the death of her daughter from cancer. Sheila's words have appeared in ChicagoNow, the Huffington Post, the *Chicago Tribune*, Scary Mommy, www.mom.me, and in the anthology *Listen To Your Mother: What She Said Then, What We're Saying Now* (2015). Her blog Mary Tyler Mom Writes focuses on themes of grief, parenting, social justice, gun violence, public education, politics, and sometimes, just to keep it light, fashion and TV shows.

Why did you choose to become a blogger?

I started writing an online journal with my husband just a few days after our daughter was diagnosed with an aggressive brain tumor. Initially it was meant to be an efficient communication tool for friends and family, updating them on our girl without needing to repeat information. She was in treatment for over two years and we sustained that journal throughout her illness. The writing was both a release and a tool. I valued the connection it provided and being able to express myself through language during a devastating experience. Giving voice to my worst fears was cathartic and helped me put those fears someplace so I could be there for my dear girl. After our daughter died, my husband stopped writing, but I continued. It turns out, having the back and forth with readers was healing and productive for my grief.

After our daughter's death, I made a conscious decision to create a blog. This was in 2011 when blogging was in its heyday. I was returning to my career in social work but didn't want to lose the connection writing had provided me. I also didn't want to keep focusing on grief, so the original intent of Mary Tyler Mom, my blogging persona, was to cover topics relevant to being a working parent. That lasted all of six months before I "outed" myself as a grieving mother and began to write about child loss as a major focus of the blog. Speaking from that place of authenticity is when I found my audience and Mary Tyler Mom really took off.

What is a typical writing day for you?

Before these current challenging days during a global pandemic, the best time to write was after I had gotten my kids off to school in the morning. Arrive home, tidy a bit or plan household errands, start thinking while doing the repetitive tasks of running a home with young children, sit down at the computer and write. Ideas are kept on the notepad of my phone so they aren't lost in the minute. I also enjoy opining on current issues or news of the day, so writing often involves research. It's not unusual for me to race the clock to publish something and crosspost on my social media channels just as I am dashing off for school dismissal. Once the kids are back home, writing gets a lot more complicated so if I miss those morning, kid-free hours, the task and demands of writing become both more complicated and less likely to be achieved.

What's the best part of your job?

I love the independence of writing—just me and the keyboard, typing away. I love creating an online community around my words. I love the challenge of capturing the nuance of something ephemeral or complicated, whether it is a thorny political issue or working to explain the pain of packing up a closet full of little girl clothes that will never be worn again because that little girl has died. When I am successful, I feel accomplished, productive, relevant, connected. The connection with readers is probably the best part of blogging. It is still surprising and humbling that strangers on the Internet take the time to read what I write and seem to care about what I have to say.

What's the worst or most challenging part of being a blogger?

As my platform expanded and my blog became more well-known, I was honored to get shots at different types of writing opportunities. It is wonderfully flattering to be recognized for my writing when writing is something that I still feel "happened" to me. It never feels like something I set out to do, but instead, something I fell into that somehow clicked. "Imposter syndrome" is a very real thing for me. Things that contribute to that are how I came to writing, that I originally gained prominence as a "mommy blogger," and that I did not become a successful blogger until well into my forties. That sense of feeling unworthy or not qualified can hinder the hustle needed to remain successful in this arena and branch out into other forms of writing like paid freelance work or content marketing.

What's the most surprising thing about being a blogger/writer?

By nature, I am shy and a wee bit insecure, though I have always had strong opinions on things and have enjoyed a good debate. Cultivating my blog has provided me a platform that has enabled me to strengthen my voice and my passionate opinions without challenging my innate shyness and insecurities. I can roar like a lion, and do, from the comfort of my dining room table. Then, inevitably, when a strong opinion about a controversial subject is expressed, someone will object. It is the nature of the beast, and honestly the mark of a successful blog. If you're doing it right, your words will provoke, but dealing with the fallout of angry readers sometimes feels above my pay grade.

Additionally, there is the potency of being thought of as an "influencer" by folks who don't know you, then turning off the computer and having a six-year-old refuse to brush his teeth or pick up his dirty socks. Kiddo! Don't you know I'm kind of a big deal on the Internet?! Children will always keep you humble.

What kinds of qualities do you think one needs to be successful at this role?

H-U-S-T-L-E is the name of the game in blogging. One of my early champions was a fellow blogger who had amassed a Facebook community around her blog of over a million followers. She and I became friendly when I was just starting out and she gave me sound advice that has never failed me, "Do the work." The work of blogging is to keep producing—keep writing, keep engaging your audience, keep flexing and growing, keep feeding that Internet content beast.

The social media landscape has changed dramatically in the past five years, with an emphasis on video (YouTube and TikTok), imagery (Instagram), and hot-take sound bites (Twitter). In some ways, blogging and all those words feel like they are from the Stone Age. But still, there is a place for words that don't involve video and require more than 280 characters (Medium is rocking). The relationship that a blogger builds with their reader is an effective tool. It is authentic, relatable, consistent, and trusted. Honor that, do the work, and success will follow.

How do you combat burnout?

I wish I knew! These past few years have kicked my blogging patootie! The world is a noisy place right now, made more so by social media and unprecedented geopolitical unrest. Adding to the drowning din often feels counterproductive and not particularly useful. I got quiet for a couple of years recently—I stopped "doing the work" required of blogging and my stats reflect that. Burnout is part of the issue, but self-preservation is part of it too. Sending controversial opinions out into the universe at this particular moment is taking a different kind of a toll that feels heavier than it used to feel.

One thing that has helped me is shifting gears. After getting quiet for a few years, I have gotten more selective and nuanced about what thoughts inside my head are deserving of my platform. I am more judicious; I read and listen more. That has helped. I have also focused on cultivating more paid writing opportunities based on melding my areas of expertise—combining my social work background, personal and professional experiences in the medical field, and writing. That is a valuable niche, it turns out, so I have enjoyed and benefited from putting the focus less on my personal opinions and more on something external to me. Finding clients that value what I can uniquely provide has helped me start doing the work of blogging once again, just in a different context.

What would you tell a young person who is thinking about becoming a blogger?
Do it! Find your passion and stay authentic. It sounds cliché, but it isn't. Learning how to craft your thoughts into your voice using words will benefit you no matter what direction your life takes you. Embrace that blogging is an endeavor that is equal parts building community and self-disclosure. When you find the right balance between those two things, it is a powerful and valuable tool.

Summary

This chapter covered a lot of ground in terms of what it is like to be a writer or an author, what the difference is between the two, and what kinds of qualities and skills being a writer or editor demands. This book focuses predominately on creative writing—fiction and creative nonfiction and poetry—because most people aspiring to earn a living writing creatively support themselves in other careers with various writing jobs and those relating to publishing. For that reason, we have considered some of the careers that an educational background and interest in creative writing will also prepare you for.

As for your future and growth as a writer or author, that is very hard to say as there are so many factors that make this uncertain. And because salaries fluctuate so much in the writing field, they are also difficult to narrow down definitively. A decline in books sales has narrowed the competitive space even more so as more people vie for fewer opportunities to earn book contracts. However, people continue to publish and seek out new writers so this should not discourage you.

Here are some ideas to take away with you as you move on to the next chapter.

- Be interested in the world around you to come up with stories that will appeal to a broad audience.
- Read, read, and read. This will help you improve your own writing.
- Have the self-discipline to work long hours outside your day job. This can be grueling so it's important to choose a project you love and believe in to help you keep going.
- Recognize that as a writer you'll have many career options available to you. You'll be able to work for various audiences, delivering different stories for different purposes.

Assuming you are now more enthusiastic than ever about pursuing a career as a writer or author, in the next chapter we'll look more closely at how you can refine your choice to a more specific job. It offers tips and advice on how to find the role and work environment that will be most satisfying to you and what steps you can start taking—immediately!—toward reaching your future career goals.

Forming a Career Plan

*C*hoosing the career you want to pursue is both very exciting and very challenging. There are so many choices available, which is the good news, but that can also make it difficult to make up your mind. Particularly if you have many passions and interests, it can be hard to narrow your options down. It is easy to feel overwhelmed especially as—no pressure—it is one of the most important decisions you will ever make.

That you are reading this book means you have decided to investigate a career as a writer or author, which means you have already discovered a passion for creativity, gathering knowledge, interacting with people, sharing and hearing stories, and continuous learning. And of course you are interested in improving and developing your ability to express yourself in written language, and you have a passion for reading.

There are many types of jobs people with strong writing skills and creativity can pursue, as we discussed in the previous chapter. This book is focused on creative writing more so than business writing, and this demands a particular lifestyle. It can mean long hours working on your own at a desk, often without knowing if you will ever sell your work (but believing that you will, which is what keeps all writers going!).

The kind of schedule and work environment that best suits you is a key factor in choosing your career path. It's a lot to think about, but fortunately it's also very exciting to consider your options particularly as it's a decision that is primarily based on aspects of you (your interests, natural gifts, curiosities) that you know more about than anyone else.

> **Tip:** This may all sound very dramatic and even scary. Keep in mind as you consider your career options that it is common to change your mind or shift gears at any stage in your career. Be thoughtful about your decisions but don't put too much pressure on yourself. It's not a case of getting only one chance to decide.

A FREELANCER'S LIFE: KEZIA ENDSLEY

Kezia Endsley.
Courtesy of Kezia Endsley.

Kezia Endsley received her bachelor's degree in journalism from Indiana University. She is a freelance nonfiction writer and editor from Indianapolis, Indiana, and has worked in publishing in one form or another for over twenty-five years. Her specialties range from editing technical publications and manuals to writing books for teens. She provides developmental, project, and copyediting for publishers and authors in various fields. In her free time, she enjoys running and triathlons, traveling, reading, and spending time with her family and pets.

What prompted you to pursue writing as a career, and how have you used your writing experience to build a career?

I always enjoyed the written word and loved reading ever since I can remember. When I went to college back in the 90s, Journalism seemed like a practical outlet for writing and editing. As fate would have it, I guess, I found myself in the book publishing field instead. I enjoyed working with authors and helping them craft their words for the benefit of their readers. As I gained experience as an editor, my desire to write in addition to editing grew. It was hard to break into writing in the technical fields because to some degree you become typecast as an editor only and not as someone who necessarily has enough product knowledge to write a book. Using some contacts I had from previous jobs, I was able to break into educational publishing as an author, specifically books for tweens and teens, which I enjoy. I think it fits my writing style nicely.

What is a typical day on the job for you?

I have been working from home as a freelancer or contractor for about twenty years. To be successful as a freelance writer (a freelance anything, really), you need to develop a routine and have discipline. My typical schedule is very morning-heavy. My best writing time is early morning before the weight of the day clogs my mind and I start thinking of all the other little things I have to do. Also, if I am behind, I'll spend morning time catching up with yesterday's work, be it writing sections of a chapter or editing someone else's material.

After getting my kids off to school, I check email and put out any fires or handle immediate needs. Then I look at my plan for the day. I always have a written plan for each day, which I build the day before as that day progresses. Then I add to it as needed. My later mornings are usually organizational in nature.

Most days, my workday is broken up by exercise—either hitting the gym or running outside. This is really important to me for sanity and physical health. I think it helps me clear my mind as well so that I can better use my brain power later in the day.

Afternoons are saved for activities such as doing research on a topic, connecting with clients and returning emails, writing status reports, and other small pieces of the job that don't require huge blocks of time.

What's the best part of your work?

Even though it does have its drawbacks, I really enjoy being a freelancer. I love the variety of the publishers I work for and the work that I do. Writing and editing are nicely complementary, and for me at least, they use different kinds of energy. That helps me stay fresh and avoid burnout. Writing is creative and it feels good to make something out of nothing, essentially. But it's hard work that requires long, intense periods of concentration. Editing someone else's work is just different. It requires attention too, of course, but it can be broken more easily into chunks.

What's the worst, or most challenging, part of your job?

As a freelancer, you are never sure when the work will dry up. Also, you tend to be last in line as far as how they treat you as an employee. Also, no benefits or healthcare. Thankfully, I have the ACA! I do worry a lot about having enough work and whether the work will dry up or move overseas.

Writer's block can also be an issue sometimes, but I combat that by having a disciplined writing schedule each day. Being a freelancer, you are essentially running your own business. That's not for the faint of heart.

What is the most surprising thing about working in a writing-related profession?

For me, the writing process is different than I expected. Maybe it's because I write nonfiction books, but it's much more about perspiration than inspiration. In other words, it takes hard work, organization, proper research, and effort. Having said that, I also find it surprising how much I enjoy the creative process. Creating something that's all your own, as opposed to editing someone else's work, feels really good.

How do you combat writer's block? How do you stay motivated and avoid burnout?

I deal with writer's block by being organized and breaking my tasks into smaller chunks. Perhaps because I write nonfiction materials, I always start by creating a detailed outline. That gives me a basic idea about the road ahead of me. Even when that outline changes, as it usually does, I find it very helpful to have a blueprint of sorts for when I get stuck. I then know what the next step is. Breaking a large job into smaller steps has always been a technique that works well for me.

I think taking breaks is also very important. And know yourself and figure out when you're most productive and creative. Get into a schedule and use that time wisely. Don't try to do your best writing when you are tired, burnt out, or preoccupied with other issues. Mainly, though, be kind to yourself. It will come in time.

What would you tell a young person who is thinking about a career in writing?

Read and write as much as you can. That might seem obvious, but I am surprised sometimes when I find that it is not. When you read something you really enjoy, fiction or nonfiction, try to figure out what it is about it that you enjoy. Of course, it's important to discover and write in your own voice. When you are starting out, no project is too small. Use these to build a portfolio or a résumé.

In the long haul, write about what interests you. If you find yourself doing something that is boring or doesn't keep you interested, it's going to feel a lot more like work than something you enjoy! Life is too short—find something you enjoy doing.

A career as a writer or author offers a lot of choice and variety. Before you can plan your path to a successful career in the industry—such as by committing to a college program—it's helpful to develop an understanding of what role you want to have and in what kind of environment you wish to work. Are you in a position financially to pursue your own creative work full-time, or will you—as most aspiring writers do—work another job while simultaneously working on your novel? What geographic choices impact your options?

It's also important to think about how much education you'd like to pursue. Depending on your career goal, the steps to getting there differ. Writing jobs, such as journalist or copywriter, typically require a bachelor's degree or higher. You can choose to study anything that relates to writing, literature, commu-

"I write to discover what I know."—Flannery O'Connor (1925–1964), American novelist, short-story writer, and essayist

nications, or another subject that is not writing-specific but will inform the writing you want to do. The choices are many, and we will look at them a bit in this chapter as well as discuss particular schools that offer programs of interest.

Deciding on a career means asking yourself big questions, but there are tools and assessment tests that can help you determine what your personal strengths and aptitudes are and which career fields and environments they best align with. These tools will guide you to think about important factors in choosing a career path such as how you respond to pressure and how effectively and how much you enjoy working and communicating with people.

YOUR PASSIONS, ABILITIES, AND INTERESTS: IN JOB FORM!

Think about how you've done at school and how things have worked out at any temporary or part-time jobs you've had so far. What are you really good at in your opinion? And what have other people told you you're good at? What are you not very good at right now but you would like to become better at? What are you not very good at and you're okay with not getting better at?

Now forget about work for a minute. In fact, forget about needing to ever have a job again. You won the lottery—congratulations. Now answer these questions: What are your favorite three ways of spending your time? For each one of those things, can you describe why you think you in particular are attracted to it? If you could get up tomorrow and do anything you wanted all day long, what would it be? These questions can be fun but can also lead you to your true passions. The next step is to find the job that sparks your passions.

This chapter explores the educational requirements for various careers within the writing world as well as options for where to go for help when planning your path to the career you want. It offers advice on how to begin preparing for your career path at any age or stage in your education, including high school.

Planning the Plan

So where to begin? Before taking the leap and applying to or committing in your mind to a particular college, there are other considerations and steps you can

Tip: Although not all writers pursue formal education after high school, if college is an option for you, pursuing a post–high school education can only benefit you. It can help sharpen your thinking and writing skills, help you better shape and convey ideas, and expose you to people and experiences.

take to map out your plan for pursuing your career. Preparing your career plan begins with developing a clear understanding of what your actual career goal is.

Planning your career path means asking yourself questions that will help you shape a clearer picture of what your long-term career goals are and what steps to take in order to achieve them. When considering these questions, it's important to prioritize your answers—when listing your skills, for example, put them in order of strongest to weakest. When considering questions relating to how you want to balance your career with the rest of your non-work life, such as family and hobbies, really think about what your top priorities are and in what order.

"If my doctor told me I had only six minutes to live, I wouldn't brood. I'd type a little faster."—Isaac Asimov (1920–1992), American writer and professor of biochemistry

The following are questions that are helpful to think about deeply when planning your career path.

- What are your interests outside the work context? How do you like to spend your free time? What inspires you? What kind of people do you like to surround yourself with, and how do you best learn? What do you really love doing? (Hint: If you find you dislike reading, being a writer may not be for you.)
- Can you make a list of the various career choices within the writing industry that you might be interested in pursuing (consider teaching, editing, or working as a journalist)? Organize the list in order of which careers you find most appealing and then list what it is about each that attracts you. This can be anything from work environment to geographic location to how much you'd work with other people and in what capacity.
- What information can you find on each job on your career choices list? You might find job descriptions, salary indications, career outlook, and educational requirements information online, for example. Some of this information was provided in chapter 1 of this book.

- What are your personality traits? This is very important to finding which jobs might "fit" you and which almost certainly will not. How do you respond to stress and pressure? How do you react to criticism and rejection? Do you work well in teams or prefer to work independently? Do you consider yourself creative? Are you curious and thorough? All of these are important to keep in mind to ensure you choose a career path that makes you happy and in which you can thrive.
- What other factors feature in your vision of your ideal life? Think about how your career will fit in with the rest of your life, including whether you want to live in a big city or small town, how much flexibility you want in your schedule, how much autonomy you want in your work, and what your ultimate career goal is.
- What are your pay expectations, now and in the future? While there are many lucrative careers relating to writing, many job opportunities that offer experience to newcomers and recent graduates come with a relatively low salary.

Posing these questions to yourself and thinking about them deeply and answering them honestly will help make your career goals clearer and guide you in knowing which steps you will need to take to get there.

A great way to narrow down the right career path for you is to ask yourself questions and really think about—and write down—your answers. Think about your strengths, your interests, what kinds of subjects or activities naturally appeal to you. This will help you shape an idea of what kind of education and work path will be right for you. *GaudiLab/iStock/Getty Images.*

It's important to remember that finding professional work as a writer or author can be tough. It's a very competitive field that, particularly when you are starting out in your career, will require you to work hard—sometimes only for experience, as in an internship—and to work long hours, take less-glamorous assignments or tasks, and not earn a particularly glowing salary. With creative writing, it means working on a project that may never see the light of day while simultaneously working another job to pay the bills, which can be discouraging. It's important to think about how willing you are to put in long hours and perform what can be very demanding work—without burning out.

Where to Go for Help

Again, the process of deciding on and planning a career path is daunting. In many ways, the range of choices of careers available today is a wonderful thing. It allows us to refine our career goals and customize them to our lives and personalities. In other ways though, too much choice can be extremely daunting and can require a lot of soul-searching to navigate clearly.

Answering questions about your habits, characteristics, interests, and personality can be very challenging. Identifying and prioritizing all of your ambitions, interests, and passions can be overwhelming and complicated. It's not always easy to see ourselves objectively or see a way to achieve what matters most to us. But there are many resources and approaches to help guide you in drawing conclusions about these important questions.

- Take a career assessment test to help you answer questions about what career best suits you. There are several available online, including tests for writing and authoring careers. For example, www.allthetests.com offers an "Are You a Writer at Heart?" quiz.[1]
- Consult with a career or personal coach who can help you refine your understanding of your goals and how to pursue them.
- Follow a local or online writing workshop in which writers of all levels share, discuss, and critique each other's work.
- Talk with professionals working in the job you are considering and ask them what they enjoy about their work, what they find the most challenging, and what path they followed to get there.

- Work on your portfolio. Don't wait until you can be paid professionally to start building a body of work, be it published or not. Start a blog, for example, or anything that shows your writing prowess and helps you develop your voice and, hopefully, an audience.

ONLINE RESOURCES TO HELP YOU PLAN YOUR PATH

The Internet is an excellent source of advice and assessment tools that can help you find and figure out how to pursue your career path. Some of these tools will focus on your personality and aptitude, others will help you identify and improve your skills to prepare for your career.

In addition to the sites below, you can use the Internet to find a career or life coach near you—many offer their services online as well. Job sites such as LinkedIn are a good place to search for people working in a profession you'd like to learn more about or to explore the types of jobs available in the writing industry.

- At www.educations.com you'll find a career test designed to help you find the job of your dreams. Visit www.educations.com/career-test to take the test.
- The *Princeton Review* has created a career quiz that focuses on personal interests: www.princetonreview.com/quiz/career-quiz.
- The BLS provides information, including quizzes and videos, to help students up to grade 12 explore various career paths. The site also provides general information on career prospects and salaries. Visit www.bls.gov to find these resources.

Note: Young adults with disabilities can face additional challenges when planning a career path. DO-IT (Disabilities, Opportunities, Internetworking, and Technology) is an organization dedicated to promoting career and education inclusion for everyone. Its website[2] contains a wealth of information and tools to help all young people plan a career path, including self-assessment tests and career exploration questionnaires.

Making High School Count

Once you have narrowed down your interests and have a fairly strong idea about what type of career you want to pursue, you naturally want to start putting your career path plan into motion as quickly as you can. If you are a high school student, you may feel there isn't much you can do toward achieving your career goals—other than, of course, earning good grades and graduating. But there are actually many ways you can make your high school years count toward your career as a writer or author before you have earned your high school diploma. This section will cover how you can use this period of your education and life to better prepare for your career goal and to keep your passion alive while improving your skillset.

Note: The good news with writing is you are never too young to start. If you have the ambition to be a writer or author, odds are you've been writing stories since you were very young and devouring the writing of others. This means you've started on your way to a career in the field of writing already and are off to an excellent start.

People who grow up to be writers and authors usually have one thing in common: They discovered a love of reading, writing, and playing with language at an early age. *cihatatceken/E+/Getty Images.*

COURSES TO TAKE IN HIGH SCHOOL

Depending on your high school and what courses you have access to, there are many subjects that will help you prepare for a career as a writer or author. Even if creative writing is your ultimate goal, any kind of writing will improve your ability to work with language and refine your craft.

If your school has a blog or newspaper, that's a very good way to gain experience as a writer or editor. You can also volunteer to work on your school's yearbook—it's a good way to learn about publishing. If there is a literary journal, that's another excellent outlet to explore your creativity. If these are not in existence at your school, consider starting a blog, newspaper, or journal yourself. It's a good way to gain experience but also to discover other people with similar interests you can learn from and who can learn from you.

> **Note:** Whether you are giving or receiving feedback, you will learn to identify strengths and weaknesses in writing, discover how to articulate what works for you in a piece of writing and what doesn't, and be able to offer and receive constructive criticism to make your work stronger.

If you go to a school that offers media and journalism courses, of course that's a good place to start as well. There are many courses that can help you prepare for a writing career. Some of them may seem unrelated initially, but they will all help you prepare and develop key skills.

- Language arts. You can't write, edit, or communicate without a strong knowledge of language. It won't hurt to know how to diagram a sentence or properly place a semicolon without a shadow of a doubt.
- Math. Even though you probably fancy yourself a word versus numbers person, you need to be sharp in both. Research requires an understanding of math—for example, how to interpret statistics and percentages and how to put them into terms a viewer, reader, or listener will understand.
- Public speaking. Obviously as a writer you mostly want to focus on the written word, but writers and poets often gain exposure by doing readings—perhaps at a local cafe or library that hosts events where the public can share their work. And if you are considering teaching writing in the future, you will definitely need public-speaking skills (and confidence).

- Interpersonal communication. This is pretty much relevant to any career you can imagine. Knowing how to communicate effectively is an undeniable asset. It will come in handy as you pitch to editors or agents or as you communicate with writers should you be an editor or agent. A lot of writing will entail interviewing subjects so this is also a key skill to have in the field.
- Business and economics. Again, this may not seem so relevant, but many writers work for themselves, which means having some understanding of how to build themselves as a brand, market themselves, and negotiate contracts.
- Search engine optimization. One of the key differences between online writing versus traditional print is how a publication draws its audience. These days, ranking high on search engines is essential to drawing traffic (read: an audience). Search-engine-optimization (SEO) prowess is definitely a must.

Gaining Work Experience

The best way to learn anything is to do it. When it comes to preparing for a career in writing, there are several options for gaining real-world experience and getting a feel for whether you are choosing the right career for you.

The one big benefit of jobs in this industry is you don't have to land a work-experience opportunity at an established publication, for example, to prove what you've got and what you can do. Rather than wait for someone to invite you to work for them, you are wise to keep working on your own, to show not only your talent but your passion. The more you write, the better you will become.

Note: There is a certain creative freedom to not writing for a specific audience or publisher: you are free to explore your own style, your own ideas—you can experiment just for yourself. You can start a blog and share your work when you feel ready, which is a great way to get feedback, or, as mentioned, join or start a writing workshop, online or in person. This can also help you build a nice portfolio of your work to share when applying to a school or for a job.

HOW TO START CREATING AN ATTENTION-GRABBING ONLINE WRITING PORTFOLIO

There are many online tools that can help you prepare your portfolio. This way you can share your best work to date by sharing one link as opposed to submitting several links to different articles or, worse, file attachments.

Throughout your career as a writer, you will be asked to share your work. It makes sense: while your résumé and educational background may showcase a lot of your achievements and qualifications for a job writing or publishing, what really speaks best for you and your skills is your actual work.

These online tools, many of which are free and some of which are not—take you through the steps of creating a site that showcases your work and enables people to respond to it if you so choose. As always online, be very careful what personal details you share! Some sites give you the option to be reached by viewers only through your site, which is preferable to giving your personal email address.

Some sites to check out:

- www.clippings.me
- www.journoportfolio.com
- https://contently.com
- https://wordpress.com
- https://muckrack.com/journalists

Keeping things offline, it's also a good idea to arrange to job shadow with a professional in the field in whichever capacity you find most interesting to you: an editor or a business writer, perhaps. This means accompanying someone to work, observing the tasks they perform, the work culture, the environment, the hours, and the intensity of the work. Talk with people you know who work in writing and publishing fields. Read and watch interviews with writers you admire.

Although an author may not want you standing behind them as they type, perhaps you can find someone who is an author who is willing to talk with you about their work process, how they work with agents and editors, and what a typical day is like for them. Attend any book readings in your local area; this is a great opportunity to ask questions of published authors directly.

GREAT BOOKS ABOUT HOW TO BE A WRITER

There are many books out there that can help you with all elements of writing from the sentence to plot development to structure. Here are just a few.

On Writing, by Stephen King. Known for his horror fiction, Stephen King is a self-taught, best-selling author who has a lot of excellent advice on writing presented in a memoir-like style.

Bird by Bird, by Anne Lamott. Novelist and nonfiction writer—as well as political activist—in this book, Anne Lamott shares her knowledge of what makes great writing.

The Artist's Way, by Julia Cameron. This best-seller is a workbook of sorts that provides exercises—such as daily writing practices—for overcoming challenges in unblocking your creativity, such as overcoming writer's block.

The Writer's Life: Writers on How They Think and Work, edited by Maria Arana. Particularly if creative nonfiction is your genre, but even if it's not, this book offers a collection of essays that appeared in the *Washington Post* section "Writing Life."

Plot and Structure, by James Scott Bell. This book is mainly aimed at fiction writers but is equally useful for writers of creative nonfiction. It describes approaches to developing plots by mapping them out in what are called *plot diagrams* and provides other tools and advice to overcome plot challenges.

Writing Down the Bones, by Natalie Goldberg. Particularly if you are having difficulty getting started with a piece of writing, this book provides you everything from ideas in how to find an inspiring place to write to the value of listening as a writer and even the specifics of the value of verbs.

Reading Like a Writer, by Francine Prose. Subtitled "A Guide for People Who Love Books and Those Who Want to Write Them," in this book Prose explores the work of some of the most enduring writers, including Virginia Woolf and Charles Dickens, to examine their individual styles.

The Writing Life, by Annie Dillard. As all writers know, writing can be difficult and frustrating, and that's what Dillard focuses on in this book—while sharing her words of wisdom and experience in how to overcome these hurdles.

The Elements of Style, by William Strunk Jr. and E. B. White. This classic writing guide has been a go-to resource for writing teachers for years. It covers everything from basic grammar to the principles of composition to developing your own style.

How to Write a Sentence and How to Read One, by Stanley Fish. A homage to the fine sentence, this book breaks down what makes a pleasurable, effective sentence. He references works from great writers including William Shakespeare and Henry James.

The Art of Fiction, by James Gardner. Billed as "Notes on Craft for Young Writers," this book is full of valuable advice for anyone who wants to write. Gardner explains the principles and techniques of good writing in a style that is both serious and entertaining.

Educational Requirements

Whatever type of job you want to pursue in media and journalism, you should expect to have to earn at minimum a four-year bachelor's degree. In other cases a master's or even a PhD is recommended. In addition there are certificate programs you can earn at your community college or online to continue or broaden your education throughout your career. Thomson Foundation (http://www.thomsonfoundation.org) offers a variety of professional development courses for people working in journalism and media, for example.

In the following sections, I discuss the considerations to keep in mind when deciding what level of education is best for you to pursue. In chapter 3, I will outline in more detail the types of programs offered and the best schools to consider should you want to pursue post–high school training and certification or an associate, bachelor's, or master's degree.

> "When it all gets too much, I just step away, have a good cry, talk with my wife or one of my sisters, drink wine, eat chocolate, get a massage, schedule therapy. Then I get back to it. Even when I want to quit, I know I can't. I'm a writer. It's how I process what's happening in my life and in the world."—Annie L. Scholl, writer and journalist.

WHY CHOOSE AN ASSOCIATE'S DEGREE?

A two-year degree—called an *associate's degree*—is sufficient to give you a knowledge base to begin your career and can form a basis should you decide to pursue a four-year degree later. Do keep in mind, though, that writing jobs are quite competitive. If you are prepared to put in the financial and time commitment to earn an associate's degree and are sure of the career goal you have set for yourself, consider earning a bachelor's instead. With so much competition out there, the more of an edge you can give yourself, the better your chances will be.

WHY CHOOSE A BACHELOR'S DEGREE?

A bachelor's degree—which usually takes four years to earn—is a requirement in most cases for a career in writing and publishing. Although it's true you *can* sell a book without having to have a college degree, it is not that common and it limits the kind of work you can find professionally to apply your writing skills. You should then be prepared to support yourself with a job that will require a degree such as teaching, editing, working as an in-house writer, or becoming an agent. And in general, the higher your degree, the better your odds are to advance in your career, which means more opportunity and, often, more compensation (as well as developing more contacts, having more work samples and experience, and so on). A more-advanced degree will also give you exposure to professors and peers who can help you grow and develop your skills and give you structure.

The difference between an associate's and a bachelor's degree is of course the amount of time each takes to complete. To earn a bachelor's degree, a candidate must complete 40 college courses, compared with 20 for an associate's. This translates to more courses completed and a deeper exploration of degree content even though similar content is covered in both.

WHY CHOOSE A MASTER'S DEGREE?

A master's degree is an advanced degree that usually takes two years to complete. A master's will offer you a chance to become more specialized and to build on the education and knowledge you gained while earning your bachelor's.

> **Note:** Even when not required, a master's degree can help you advance in your career, give you an edge over the competition in the field, and give you more specific knowledge relating to your work in the writing industry. It can also further hone your skills as a creative writer as well as help you make contacts with published writers, agents, and editors.

A master's can be earned directly after your bachelor's although many people choose to work for a while in between in order to discover what type of master's degree will be most relevant to their career and interests. Many people also earn their master's degree while working full- or part-time.

> **Note:** When considering a master's degree, there are many options, including what is called a master's of fine arts (MFA). These degrees are specific to creative pursuits so an MFA in writing will put the academic emphasis entirely on writing workshops and courses that support the craft of writing.

In some careers, a PhD may be required, depending on your goals. For example, if you want to pursue an academic career as a professor of literature, a PhD is generally necessary. But you can enter into the field of teaching writing without a doctorate.

DEDICATED TO THE WRITING LIFE

Nicole VanderLinden.
Courtesy of Nicole VanderLinden.

Nicole VanderLinden began writing stories at a young age, and in grade school she enticed readers by naming characters after her classmates. Once she was an adult, she received her MFA in creative writing (fiction emphasis) from Colorado State University and has since continued writing and publishing in various journals while channeling her love of words into an editing career. She's also taught creative writing, literature, and composition at the college level.

How have you used your writing experience to build a career?

When I was getting my MFA, I had the good fortune to serve as an intern at *Colorado Review*, a literary journal. In many MFA programs, there's this idea that you're being trained in the craft of writing but that you're also preparing for one of two main career paths: teaching and editing. I've done and enjoyed both, but my time at *Colorado Review* taught me to love words at this really granular level. I learned how to copyedit and proofread and even do some typesetting on top of helping find strong stories for our issues. It was an invaluable experience and, I think, most directly led to my wanting to be an editor after graduating. That said, there are lots of other paths to becoming an editor, too.

What is a typical day on the job for you?

A lot of the editing and writing I do is freelance, usually for publishing companies specializing in educational materials. When I have a project, I might spend a few hours each day reading over pieces that others have written and suggesting changes to make them the best they can be. I try to make sure the ideas are clearly communicated, that there's a sense of organization, and that the piece is meeting its own purpose. I'll talk with the author too for their ideas or with editors at the companies I'm working for to make sure I'm delivering what they've asked.

These days, I also spend a lot of time serving as a volunteer reader or editor for literary magazines. This work doesn't pay but it's invaluable to helping me stay connected with literary fiction. And, of course, I try to reserve at least a small portion of each day for thinking about or actually writing my novel and other personal projects.

What's the best part of your job?

When you work with words, you can be really nimble. You can learn about new subjects and, through editing, you can become exposed to cool work you might not have read otherwise and play a role in making that work even better. If you go the instructor route, you can teach students how to love words as much as you do. You can serve as a reader and help decide what gets published at magazines or presses—and I must say, rooting for a story you love is very exciting. And, of course, through it all, you can continue reading and writing for your own personal projects.

What's the worst or most challenging part about writing and editing?

Balance is always a challenge. There's this myth that to live the writing life you have to dedicate huge chunks of time every single day, which just isn't realistic for many of us. But on the other hand, it's easy to let personal writing projects rank last in the day-to-day list of priorities. Clients have deadlines, after all, and there are family needs, social obligations, laundry, etc., as well. But it truly doesn't have to (and perhaps even shouldn't) be all or nothing, even if your brain sometimes tells you that it does. In my experience, the best way around this is to set a realistic process for yourself, but then once you do, make it a priority to honor that process. You can have a rich editing or teaching career and a fulfilling life as a creative writer at the same time, and one can support the other, but you need to be intentional about it.

What's the most surprising thing about writing and editing?

Time and time again, I've been impressed with how marketable a solid grasp of language can be. Any field that has written material has a need for editors, for example. This goes back to this idea that editors can be nimble, and it's so true—in many ways, words open up the world.

What kinds of qualities do you think one needs to be successful at working with words?

I think writing, editing, and teaching are all best done in a state of high curiosity. It also helps to occupy this sweet spot between being a grammarian—knowing the rules of language—and understanding that almost every rule can be broken in the right context. Also, knowing what you want to say is important, of course, but so is developing an awareness of what other people are trying to say, and how you can best help them get there.

How do you combat writer's block?

Some people think writer's block exists, and others don't; for me, the question is almost irrelevant because what's most important is that I'm listening to myself. Some days I'm working with words on the page, and when I do, that's great. But other days, I'm just not there yet, and if I forced it, it wouldn't work out well. That's just me. Instead, I'll take a walk and think about the big picture, or I'll go to a place that's unfamiliar to me, because to write, of course, you also have to experience, and experience can jog new ideas. Or I'll read about the craft of writing, which sometimes helps.

What would you tell a young person who is thinking about a career in writing?

I would say, believe in your work. Keep at it, and if you love stories, remember that it's a big world out there. You can read for journals, write book reviews, teach writing, edit writing, and so much more. Also, don't be afraid to put yourself out there. I'm part of a Facebook group where we actually celebrate our rejections from journals, presses, and agents because that means we're trying. And in this business, there's no success without some measure of rejection—that's just the way it is. But there's beauty in that, too, because this means you're always reaching, always growing.

Summary

This chapter covered a lot of ground in terms of how to break down the challenge of not only discovering what career within the writing industry is right for you and in what environment, capacity, and work culture you want to work but also how best to prepare yourself for achieving your career goal.

In this chapter, we looked at the various types of jobs that are available to a writer and in publishing in general. The chapter also pointed to many tools and methods that can help you navigate the confusing path to choosing a career that is right for you. It also addressed some of the specific training and educational options and requirements and expectations that will put you, no matter what your current education level or age, at a strong advantage in a competitive field.

Use this chapter as a guideline for how to best discover what type of career will be the right fit for you and consider what steps you can already be taking to get there. Some tips to leave you with:

- Take time to carefully consider what kind of work environment you see yourself working in and what kind of schedule, interaction with colleagues, work culture, and responsibilities you want to have.
- Have a writer's ear: there are stories all around you. Writers are not just excellent wordsmiths but keen listeners.
- Job-shadow a professional to get a feeling for what hours they keep, what challenges they face, and what the overall job entails. Find out what education or training they completed before launching their career.
- Look for online or local writing workshops or venues that host public events where people can read their work to an audience. Whether you listen or participate, it will give you exposure to more writing and to more people who write.
- Don't feel you have to wait until you graduate from high school to begin taking steps to accomplish your career goals. The more you write and read, the stronger a writer you will become.
- Keep you work-life balance in mind. The career you choose will be one of many adult decisions you make, and ensuring that you keep all of your priorities—family, location, work schedule—in mind will help you choose the right career for you, which will make you a happier person.

In chapter 3, we go into detail about the types of degrees you can pursue post–high school so you can explore which is right for you. It will help you refine what type of degree you want, what type of school is a good fit, which are some of the best schools offering programs in your area of interest, and, of course, how to pay for it all.

3

Pursuing the Education Path

*M*aking decisions about your education path can be just as daunting as choosing a career path. It is a decision that not only demands understanding what kind of education or training is required for the career you want but also what kind of school or college you want to attend. There is a lot to consider no matter what area of study you want to pursue or what type of job you want to have within the written arts.

Now that you've gotten an overview of the different degree options that can prepare you for your future career as a writer or author, this chapter will dig more deeply into how to best choose the right type of study for you. Even if you are years away from earning your high school diploma or equivalent, it's never too soon to start weighing your options, thinking about the application process, and of course taking time to really consider what kind of educational track and environment will suit you best.

You may be thinking that as your career goal is a creative one, the best use of your time after high school is not to spend more years in a classroom but to just get straight to the writing. While there is truth to the idea that life is the best classroom, consider that college can also provide experiences that will help you as a writer and a thinker in a multitude of ways, from providing structure through assignments and deadlines (it's a good way to learn the discipline required as a writer) to exposure to people and ideas that can inform your writing. And of course college can be a unique and memorable life experience that will give you all the more to write about.

On a more practical level, jobs in publishing such as being an editor or agent and jobs in business writing such as copywriting and technical writing will require a college degree. Even if one of these is not your career goal, keep in mind that you may find yourself funding your creative ambitions with such jobs.

Not everyone wants to take time to go to college or pursue other forms of academic-based training. But if you are interested in following the education path—from earning a certificate in writing or editing to a four-year degree or higher—this chapter will help you navigate the process of deciding on the type of institution you would most thrive in, determine what type of degree you want to earn, and look into costs and how to find help in meeting them.

> **Note:** According to the National Center for Education Statistics (NCES), six years after entering college for an undergraduate degree only 60 percent of students have graduated.[1] Barely half of those students will graduate from college in their lifetime.[2]

It's never been more important to get your degree. College graduates with a bachelor's degree typically earn 66 percent more than those with only a high school diploma and are also far less likely to face unemployment. Also, over the course of a lifetime, the average worker with a bachelor's degree will earn approximately $1 million more than a worker without a postsecondary education.[3]

This chapter will also give you advice on the application process, how to prepare for any entrance exams that you may need to take such as the SAT or ACT, and how to communicate your passion, ambition, and personal experience in a personal statement. When you've completed this chapter, you should have a good sense of what kind of post–high school education is right for you and know how to ensure you have the best chance of being accepted at the institution of your choice.

> "You should write because you love the shape of stories and sentences and the creation of different words on a page. Writing comes from reading, and reading is the finest teacher of how to write."—Annie Proulx (1935), American novelist, short-story writer, and journalist

Finding a Program or School That Fits Your Personality

Before we get into the details of good schools that offer degrees in subjects related to writing, it's a good idea for you to take some time to consider what

CONSIDERING A GAP YEAR

Taking a year off between high school and college, often called a *gap year*, is normal, perfectly acceptable, and almost required in many countries around the world, and it is becoming increasingly acceptable in the United States as well. Particularly if you want to pursue a career as a writer, exposure to the world outside the classroom will help you gain perspective and experience that you can immediately apply to your future work. Because the cost of college has gone up dramatically, it literally pays for you to know going in what you want to study, and a gap year—well spent—can do lots to help you answer that question. It can also give you an opportunity to explore different places and people and get a deeper sense of what you'd like to study when your gap year has ended. A gap year can help you see things from a new perspective.

Some great ways to spend your gap year include joining the Peace Corps or another organization that offers work-experience opportunities. Or you might consider enrolling in a mountaineering program or another gap year–styled program; for example, you might backpack across Europe or other countries on the cheap (be safe and bring a friend); find a volunteer organization that furthers a cause you believe in or that complements your career aspirations; join a Road Scholar program (see www.roadscholar.org); teach English in another country (see www.gooverseas.com/blog/best-countries-for-seniors-to-teach-english-abroad); or work and earn money for college!

Many students will find that they get much more out of college when they have a year to mature and to experience the real world. The American Gap Year Association reports from their alumni surveys that students who take a gap year show improved civic engagement, improved college graduation rates, and improved college GPAs. See their website, https://gapyearassociation.org/, for lots of advice and resources if you're considering a potentially life-altering experience.

type of school might be best for you. Just as with your future work environment, understanding how you best learn, what type of atmosphere best fits your personality, and how and where you are most likely to succeed will play a major part in how happy you will be with your choice. This section will provide some thinking points to help you discover what kind of school or program should be the best fit for you.

If nothing else, answering questions like the following can help you narrow your search and focus on a smaller sampling of choices. Write your answers to these questions down somewhere where you can refer to them often such as in a notes app on your phone.

- *Size*: Does the size of the school matter to you? Colleges and universities range from 500 or fewer students to more than 25,000. If you are considering college or university, think about what size of class you would like and what the right instructor-to-student ratio might be for you.
- *Community location:* Would you prefer to be in a rural area, a small town, a suburban area, or a large city? How important is the location of the school in the larger world to you? Is the flexibility of an online degree or certification program attractive to you or do you prefer on-site, hands-on instruction?
- *Length of study:* How many months or years do you want to put into your education before you start working professionally?
- *Housing options:* If applicable, what kind of housing would you prefer? Dorms, off-campus apartments, and private homes are all common options.
- *Student body:* How would you like the student body to "look"? Think about coed versus all-male and all-female settings as well as the makeup of minorities, how many students are part-time versus full-time, and the percentage of commuter students.
- *Academic environment:* Consider which majors are offered and at which degree levels. Research the student-to-faculty ratio. Are the classes often taught by actual professors or more often by teaching assistants? Find out how many internships the school typically provides to students. Are independent study or study-abroad programs available in your area of interest?
- *Financial aid availability/cost:* Does the school provide ample opportunities for scholarships, grants, work-study programs, and the like? How big a part will cost play in your choice?
- *Support services:* Investigate the strength of the academic and career placement counseling services of the school.
- *Social activities and athletics:* Does the school offer clubs that you are interested in? Which sports are offered?
- *Special programs:* Does the school offer honors programs or programs for veterans or students with disabilities or special needs?

Note: Not all of these questions are going to be important to you, and that's fine. Be sure to make a note of aspects that don't matter so much to you too such as size or location. You might change your mind as you go to visit colleges, but it's important to know where you are to begin with.

MAKE THE MOST OF CAMPUS VISITS

If it's at all practical and feasible, you should visit the campuses of all the schools you're considering. To get a real feel for any college or university, you need to walk around the campus, spend some time in the common areas where students hang out, and sit in on a few classes. You can also sign up for campus tours, which are typically given by current students. This is another good way to see the campus and ask questions of someone who knows. Be sure to visit the specific campus or building that covers your possible major as well. The website and brochures won't be able to convey that intangible feeling you'll get from a visit.

Make a list of all the questions that are important to you before you visit. And in addition to the questions listed above, consider these questions as well.

- What is the makeup of the current freshman class? Is the campus diverse?
- What is the meal plan like? What are the food options?
- Where do most of the students hang out between classes? (Be sure to visit this area.)
- How long does it take to walk from one end of the campus to the other?
- What types of transportation are available for students? Does campus security provide escorts to cars, dorms, and so forth at night?

In order to be ready for your visit and make the most of it, consider these tips and words of advice. Before you go,

- be sure to do some research and make a list of questions. At the least, spend some time on the college website. Make sure your questions aren't addressed adequately there first.
- arrange to meet with a professor in your area of interest or to visit the specific school.
- be prepared to answer questions about yourself and why you are interested in this school.
- dress in neat, clean, casual clothes. Avoid overly wrinkled clothing or anything with stains.
- listen and take notes.
- don't interrupt.
- be positive and energetic.
- make eye contact when someone speaks directly to you.
- ask questions.
- thank people for their time.

Finally, be sure to send thank-you notes or emails after the visit is over. Remind the recipient of when you visited the campus and thank them for their time.

Given the current coronavirus pandemic, it is possible you will attend many of your courses online. However, many of the above points will still apply such as the student-to-faculty ratio and the diversity of the student body.

U.S. News & World Report[4] puts it best when they say the college that fits you best is one that does all these things:

- offers a degree that matches your interests and needs
- provides a style of instruction that matches the way you like to learn
- provides a level of academic rigor to match your aptitude and preparation
- offers a community that feels like home to you
- values you for what you do well

Hopefully this section has impressed upon you the importance of finding the right fit in your chosen learning institution. Take some time to paint a mental picture of the kind of university or school setting that might best complement your needs. Now read on for specifics about each degree.

> **Note:** In the academic world accreditation matters and is something you should consider when choosing a school. Accreditation is basically a seal of approval that schools promote to let prospective students feel sure the institution will provide a quality education that is worth their investment and will help them reach their career goal. Future employers will want to see that the program you completed has such a seal of quality so it's something to keep in mind when choosing a school.

Determining Your Education Plan

There are many options when it comes to pursuing an education in the writing field. These include two-year community colleges, four-year colleges, and master's programs including MFA degrees. This section will focus on undergraduate, or bachelor's, programs that can help you prepare for your career as a writer or author.

Whether you opt for a two-year or four-year degree—and possibly later a master's—you will find there are many choices. It's a good idea to select roughly 5–10 schools in a realistic location (for you) that offer the degree you want to earn. If you are considering online programs, include these in your list.

HOW TO HAVE A GAP YEAR DURING A PANDEMIC

Although we've already explored options for spending a gap year that would certainly offer you invaluable experience as an aspiring writer, currently these are not all viable options due to the coronavirus—but that does not mean there aren't enriching activities and pursuits you can engage in to make your gap year just as worthwhile.

Next Advisor[5] offers tips on how to make the most of a gap year even if it is not possible to participate in a structured program such as the Peace Corps. While these options may not seem as exciting as traveling abroad, the point of a gap year is to help you refine your interests and gain additional skills before committing to a college program. Here are some options to consider.

- Learn a new skill. Learn a new language. Become an expert in building an online audience. Take a photography course. This will be a good time to really develop yourself in new areas that may directly or indirectly affect you as a writer. And of course you should take time to write or dedicate time to researching a subject you want to write about.
- Get a job to earn money for college. The virus has hit many hard financially so taking a year to earn money before heading off to school is certainly a valuable use of your time.
- Volunteer. There are virtual volunteer programs (check out www.volunteer match.org) or you can do local volunteering such as buying groceries for an elderly neighbor.
- Seek out remote internships. Most people are currently working at home and there are opportunities for interns to do the same.
- Take online classes at a local community college. And as writing is your ambition, seek out online literature and writing courses as well as writing communities that allow you to share your work and read the work of others.

Tip: Consider attending a university in your resident state, if possible, which will save you lots of money if you attend a state school. Private institutions don't typically discount resident student tuition costs.

Note: If you are planning to apply to a college or program that requires the ACT or SAT, advisors recommend that you take both the ACT and SAT test during your junior year of high school (spring at the latest). You can retake these tests and use your highest score so be sure to leave time to retake early in your senior year if needed. You want your best score to be available to all the schools you're applying to by January of your senior year. Keep in mind these are general timelines—be sure to check the exact deadlines and calendars of the schools you're applying to!

Be sure you research the basic GPA and SAT or ACT requirements of each school as well. Although some community colleges do not require standardized tests for the application process, others do.

Once you have found 5–10 schools in a realistic location that offer the degree you want, spend some time on their websites studying the requirements for admission. Important factors weighing on your decision of which schools to apply to should include whether or not you meet the requirements; your chances of getting in (but aim high!); tuition cost and availability of scholarships and grants; location; and the school's reputation and licensure and graduation rates.

Note: Most colleges and universities will list the average stats for the last class accepted to each program, which will give you a sense of your chances of acceptance.

The order of these characteristics will depend on your grades and test scores, your financial resources, work experience, and other personal factors. Taking everything into account, you should be able to narrow your list down to the institutes or schools that best match your educational or professional goals as well as your resources and other factors such as location and duration of study.

"The purpose of a writer is to keep civilization from destroying itself."—Albert Camus (1913–1960), French philosopher, author, and journalist

Schools to Consider When Pursuing a Career as a Writer or Author

Some schools and programs have stronger reputations than others. Although you can certainly have a successful and satisfying career and experience without going to the "Number 1" school in your field of study, it is a good idea to shop around and to compare different schools to get a sense of what they offer and what features of each are the most important to you.

> **Note:** The following sections focus on institutions offering four-year bachelor's degree programs. If you are interested in pursuing an associate's degree, check with your local community college for programs offered.

Keep in mind that what is "great" for one person may not be as great for someone else. What might be the perfect school for you might be too difficult, too expensive, or not rigorous enough for someone else. Keep in mind the advice of the previous sections when determining what you really need in a school.

GREAT SCHOOLS FOR CREATIVE WRITING

If you are eager to launch your career as a writer, you should consider earning a degree that will hone your creative writing skills and understanding of the principles and techniques of good writing.

> "When I was getting my MFA, I had the good fortune to serve as an intern at Colorado Review, a literary journal. In many MFA programs, there's this idea that you're being trained in the craft of writing but that you're also preparing for one of two main career paths: teaching and editing. I've done and enjoyed both, but my time at Colorado Review taught me to love words at this really granular level."—Nicole VanderLinden, freelance editor, journal reviewer, and author of short fiction

This list of the best schools offering undergraduate programs in creative writing has been compiled by the Koppelman Group.[6]

- Columbia University, New York
- Emory University, Atlanta, Georgia
- Washington University, St. Louis, Missouri
- Princeton University, Princeton, New Jersey
- Middlebury College, Middlebury, Vermont
- Emerson College, Boston, Massachusetts
- Cornell University, Ithaca, New York
- Hamilton College, Clinton, New York
- Bucknell University, Lewisburg, Pennsylvania
- Kenyon College, Gambier, Ohio

GREAT SCHOOLS FOR ENGLISH

As an undergrad you may choose not to focus entirely on creative writing but to pursue an English degree instead while taking as many creative writing courses as you can along the way.

This list of the best schools offering undergraduate programs in creative writing has been compiled by Niche.com.[7]

- Brown University, Providence, Rhode Island
- Harvard University, Cambridge, Massachusetts
- Columbia University, New York
- University of Miami, Miami, Florida
- Stanford University, Stanford, California
- Princeton University, Princeton, New Jersey
- Yale University, New Haven, Connecticut
- Johns Hopkins University, Baltimore, Maryland
- Rice University, Houston, Texas
- University of Chicago, Chicago, Illinois

WHAT'S IT GOING TO COST YOU?

So the bottom line: What will your education end up costing you? First, some good news. According to *U.S. News & World Report*, the average tuition

School can be an expensive investment but there are many ways to find help paying for your education. *designer491/iStock/Getty Images.*

WRITING A GREAT PERSONAL STATEMENT FOR ADMISSION

The *personal statement* you include with your application to college is extremely important. This is especially true if your GPA or SAT/ACT scores are on the border of what is typically accepted. Write something that is thoughtful and conveys your understanding of the profession you are interested in as well as your desire to practice in this field. Why are you uniquely qualified? Why are you a good fit for this university? Your essay should be highly personal (hence the "personal" in "personal statement"). Will the admissions professionals who read it, along with hundreds of others, come away with a snapshot of who you really are and what you are passionate about?

Look online for examples of good ones. This will give you a feel for what works. Be sure to check your specific school for length guidelines, format requirements, and any other guidelines they expect you to follow.

And of course, be sure to proofread it several times then ask a professional (such as your school writing center or your local library services) to proofread it as well.

cost for colleges has fallen, which goes against the usual trend of costs going up each year. For private colleges, costs have fallen by about 5 percent; for in-state colleges, the costs have fallen by 4 percent, and that of out-of-state (tuition for a person attending a state school but not in their resident state) has fallen by 6 percent.[8]

In addition, there are financial aid options to help you find the funding to earn the degree you want. We cover those next.

Financial Aid: Finding Money for Education

Finding enough money to attend college can seem almost impossible at first. But you can do it if you have a plan before you actually start applying to colleges. If you get into your top-choice university, don't let the sticker cost turn you away. Financial aid can come from many different sources and it's available to cover all the different kinds of costs you'll encounter during your years in college including tuition, fees, books, housing, and food.

The good news is that universities more often offer incentive or tuition discount aid to encourage students to attend. The market is often more competitive in favor of the student, and colleges and universities are responding by offering more-generous aid packages to a wider range of students than they used to. Here are some basic tips and pointers on the financial aid process.

- You apply for financial aid during your senior year in high school. You must fill out the FAFSA (Free Application for Federal Student Aid) form at www.studentaid.gov, which can be filed starting October 1 of your senior year until June of the year you graduate. Because the amount of available aid is limited, it's best to apply as soon as you possibly can. See www.fafsa.gov to get started.
- Be sure to compare deals you get at different schools. There is room to negotiate with universities. The first offer for aid may not be the best you'll get.
- Wait until you receive all offers from your top schools and then use this information to negotiate with your top choice to see if they will match or beat the best aid package you've received.

- To be eligible to keep and maintain your financial aid package, you must meet certain grade or GPA requirements. Be sure you are very clear on these academic expectations and keep up with them.
- You must reapply for federal aid every year.

Note: Watch out for scholarship scams! You should never be asked to pay to submit the FAFSA form ("Free" is in its name) or be required to pay to find appropriate aid and scholarships. These are free services. If an organization promises you you'll get aid or that you have to "act now or miss out," these are both warning signs of a less-reputable organization.

Also be careful with your personal information to avoid identity theft as well. Simple things like closing and exiting your browser after visiting sites where you've entered personal information can be very effective. And don't share your student aid ID number with anyone either.

It's important to understand the different forms of financial aid that are available to you. That way you'll know how to apply for different kinds of aid and you'll get the financial aid package that best fits your needs and strengths. The two main categories that financial aid falls under are *gift aid* (which doesn't have to be repaid) and *self-help aid* (which are either loans that must be repaid or work-study funds that are earned). The next sections cover the various types of financial aid that fit in one of these areas.

GRANTS

Grants typically are awarded to students who have financial needs but can also be awarded in the areas of athletics, academics, demographics, veteran support, and special talents. They do not have to be paid back. Grants can come from federal agencies, state agencies, specific universities, and private organizations. Most federal and state grants are based on financial need.

Examples of grants are the Pell Grant, SMART Grant, and the Federal Supplemental Educational Opportunity Grant (FSEOG). Visit the U.S. Department of Education's Federal Student Aid site for lots of current information about grants (https://studentaid.ed.gov/types/grants-scholarships).

SCHOLARSHIPS

Scholarships are merit-based aid that does not have to be paid back. They are typically awarded based on academic excellence or some other special talent such as in music or art. Scholarships also fall under the areas of athletic-based, minority-based, aid for women, and so forth. These are typically not awarded by federal or state governments but instead come from the specific university you applied to as well as private and nonprofit organizations.

Be sure to reach out directly to the financial aid officers of the schools you want to attend. These people are great contacts who can lead you to many more sources of scholarships and financial aid. Visit www.gocollege.com/financial-aid/scholarships/types/ for lots more information about how scholarships in general work.

LOANS

Many types of loans are available to students to pay for their post-secondary education. However, the important thing to remember here is that loans must be paid back, with interest. Be sure you understand the interest rate you will be charged. This is the extra cost of borrowing the money and is usually a percentage of the amount you borrow. Is the rate fixed or will it change over time? Is repayment of the loan and interest deferred until you graduate (meaning you don't have to begin paying the loan off until after you graduate)? Is the loan subsidized (meaning the federal government pays the interest until you graduate)? These are all points you need to be clear about before you sign on the dotted line.

There are many types of loans offered to students, including need-based loans, non-need-based loans, state loans, and private loans. Two very reputable federal loans are the Perkins Loan and the Direct Stafford Loan. For more information about student loans, start at https://bigfuture.collegeboard.org/pay-for-college/loans/types-of-college-loans.

FEDERAL WORK-STUDY

The U.S. Federal Work-Study program provides part-time jobs for undergraduate and graduate students with financial need so they can earn money to pay for educational expenses. The focus of such work is on community service work and work related to a student's course of study. Not all colleges and universities participate in this program so be sure to check with the school financial aid office if this is something you are counting on. The sooner you apply, the more likely you will get the job you desire and be able to benefit from the program as funds are limited. For more information about this opportunity see https://studentaid.ed.gov/sa/types/work-study.

GENERAL FINANCIAL AID TIPS

- Some colleges and universities offer tuition discounts to encourage students to attend—so tuition costs can be lower than they look at first.
- Apply for financial aid during your senior year of high school. The sooner you apply, the better your chances.
- Compare offers from different schools—one school may be able to match or improve on another school's financial aid offer.
- Keep your grades up—a good GPA helps a lot when it comes to merit scholarships and grants.
- You have to reapply for financial aid every year, so you'll be filling out that FAFSA form again!
- Look for ways that loans might be deferred or forgiven—service commitment programs are a way to use service to pay back loans.

GEORGE GUIDA: POET AND MORE

George Guida.
Courtesy of George Guida.

George Guida started writing poems and stories when he was twelve years old. In high school he decided that he would try to become a writer. He edited his high school newspaper and after graduation attended Columbia University, where he majored in English, edited the Columbia Guide to New York, and wrote for several campus publications. He published his first work—poems, stories, and journalistic essays—in small literary journals in the late 1980s as an undergraduate and then as a doctoral student at the City University of New York, where he earned his PhD in English. He has taught literature and creative writing at New York City College of Technology since 1998. During his professional life, he has also served as poetry editor for *2 Bridges Review*; treasurer of the Italian American Writers Association; president of the Italian American Studies Association; and curator of several poetry-reading series around New York State. He has published eight books, including a collection of short fiction, two collections of essays, and five collections of poems, most recently *Zen of Pop* and *New York and Other Lovers*. He is currently in the late stages of writing a novel called "The Uniform" and in the early stages of writing a long-researched book on communities of poets around the United States called "Virtue at the Coffee House."

How have you used your writing experience to build a career?

Once I discovered that I liked to write, the question really was, how could I find a career to support my writing habit? My first thought was to get a degree in law or journalism, either of which would allow me to use my writing skills while helping me to improve those skills. So I took lots of English courses, thought about taking history courses, and wrote for my college newspaper. By the time I reached my final year of college, I realized that I was a decent literary critic and a limited, but maybe promising, creative writer. I also realized that I might not be cut out for journalism (too much travel) or law (too much time in an office). At that point I didn't know what to do so I decided to delay the decision by getting a graduate degree in English. I applied to one program in creative writing, which didn't accept me, and a few in critical studies, which did. I chose the City University of New York's Doctoral English Program because it had a solid reputation and because they were willing to give me free tuition plus a scholarship and teaching stipend. They were impressed with the Ivy League name on my résumé, which justified the trouble and expense of attending an Ivy League college in the first place. Now, as I tell my students, the name of the undergraduate institution isn't worth nearly as much. It's the graduate degree that counts.

In graduate school I discovered that I truly enjoyed researching and writing essays about literature and culture, an interest that sealed my professional fate. I would be a professor. A professor's life, like a student's, derives from writing, and allows for time to write. Once I finished writing my critical essays and grading papers for my job as an adjunct instructor, I had plenty of hours left over to write poems, though maybe not enough time to write the novels I had always thought I would write. Still, I had a satisfying professional and writing life in New York City, complete with a circle of writer friends and lots of readings and events. In both my academic career and literary career, my writing was my passport. During this period I slowly gained respect as a writer and scholar, published some work, and made friends and acquaintances who were a significant part of my professional and personal life for the next twenty-five years.

What is a typical day on the job for you?

When you teach, especially at the college level, no two work days are alike. We faculty members at New York City College of Technology have "assigned days," days we are required to be on campus. Most faculty members at my college have anywhere from two to four of these each week, depending on their schedule of classes and service on different department, college, and university committees. Committee meetings are the X factor, creating variation in schedules from week to week. "Unassigned days" have whatever structure the individual instructor gives them.

I typically teach three partly online courses each semester. Each class meets once per week, which means I am generally on campus two or three days each week, teaching a total of five hours in the classroom. On those days and on unassigned days I will usually grade or prepare for upcoming classes. Preparation takes about twice the time that actually classroom teaching does, but grading is the most time-consuming of the tasks. I will often spend thirty hours each week grading, if not more. Of course these weekly hours do not include the time it takes to build a course and create assignments. That work happens prior to each semester. Building each course requires at least one full week's work, anywhere from thirty to forty hours, less if I am just making adjustments to an existing course.

Some days during the semester I will have time to conduct research or to write. I focus now mostly on writing poetry and fiction, but I've written many critical essays and reviews, and a couple of plays. I like to write for at least two hours at a time, especially when I'm writing fiction or essays, both of which involve on-the-spot research and linking different parts of a larger whole. In other words, prose writing requires keeping other parts of a piece you are working on constantly in mind. Poetry can also demand those sorts of mental gymnastics, but a draft or revision of a poem can happen within an hour or in several shorter bursts as most poems, at least most lyric poems, are relatively limited in their scope. Writing also occasionally requires time to send work to journals and publishers, which in turn requires manuscript preparation. That work can be tedious, but it is not as mentally taxing as the actual writing. Of course I write a great deal between the periods when I am teaching, and I certainly limit research trips to those times, usually on short breaks or between semesters.

I should add that for years I have had a second job, teaching fully online writing classes at Walden University. Those classes require only grading, no preparation, but they do run all year and can take up to ten hours each week. When you teach online, you need to check in regularly and have a weekly rhythm to post replies and assignment feedback, so I would say that discipline matters a great deal in online teaching, and, really, in teaching of any sort. You need to be self-motivated to get your work done and to successfully engage students on a regular basis.

What's the best part of your work as a professor and writer?

The best part of teaching is, as most teachers will tell you, working with students in the classroom. Classroom discussions, good ones, create a synergy of ideas that is both stimulating and, in a positive way, exhausting. I often feel spent at the end of a classroom session, which is very much like a performance, at least if it is a successful class. Even as a "guide on the side" (as opposed to a "sage on the stage," a teacher who lectures most of the time), I have to be engaged and engaging, fully present and ready for surprises. Students will ask questions I haven't prepared to answer or questions that require lengthy and delicate discussion. In either case, I have to work hard to maintain class interest and mutual respect.

I'm not sure I can pick a best part of writing. I love writing above all other tasks, as difficult as it is. I enjoy brainstorming and planning a piece almost as much as I enjoy those periods of creative energy when the ideas and lines just seem to flow from the brain and heart onto the page or screen. And I enjoy the process of revision, of finding and repairing, or removing, the weak spots in a piece.

What's the worst or most challenging part of your job as a professor and writer?

The most challenging part of teaching is, without doubt, offering feedback on assignments. Grading and commenting tend to be repetitive exercises since assignments can produce similar responses from students. Commenting on student responses, whether they are argumentative essays or poems, takes time (upward of a half-hour per essay or poem) and concentration, and often it doesn't produce the desired effect of great improvement upon revision. The truth is that improving one's writing takes time so the instructor has to savor small bits of student progress over the course of a semester or the course of a student's entire academic career.

Teaching at the college level also involves attending a lot of committee meetings. While these meetings sometimes produce important results, such as new courses or majors and services for students, they can also drag on and produce few results. They are necessary but can lack direction and urgency and can be rife with squabbling.

The most challenging part of being a writer is accepting rejection as a part of professional life. For the first ten years of my career as a writer, I would guess that ninety percent of the poems and stories I submitted for publication received rejection notices. From my work as an editorial intern at the *Paris Review* and the *Hudson Review*, and from my more recent work as poetry editor of *2 Bridges Review*, I know that that percentage is typical for writers, especially for new and emerging writers. If you can accept these rejections and learn to focus on the acceptances, the publications, and the public readings as connections with your audience and with other writers, you will enjoy literary success if not necessarily a great income from writing.

What is the most surprising thing about teaching and editing?

The most surprising thing about college-level teaching is how much of the work is solitary. I spend thirty to forty hours each week preparing for classes, commenting on student work, and writing documents as part of committee and administrative tasks. I spend fewer than twenty hours actually interacting with students and other instructors.

The most surprising thing about writing is how the solitary practice of writing can be the basis for a lifetime of public performance, for entry into fulfilling social and professional circles of acquaintances, and for lasting friendships. For three decades now I've had the pleasure of giving public readings and talks and of befriending dozens of writers and other intellectuals, some of whom have become my closest friends and confidants.

How do you combat writer's block?

I don't believe in writer's block. It's not that I'm not self-conscious to stymie my own progress. I've spent plenty of time worrying about what other people think of me. It's just that I realized at a fairly young age that no one is out there waiting for my next publication. If a few people read and enjoy it, I've done my job. If they come up to me in person or comment on social media that my writing has moved them, that's a bonus, and one of the great joys of being a writer. The best writing, I think, comes from what we want or need to write, from the desire to engage in the writing process, and from trusting your instincts to follow certain ideas. Keeping journals of ideas and notes has helped me to trust in my ideas and in my process of developing them. If I have no ideas to pursue at a given time, I give myself a break and do other things for a while. Most people are busy, so taking breaks from writing is usually a relief and a great means of rejuvenating the creative mind. If I'm having trouble conceiving a given project, I sometimes turn to another project as a way to keep writing without getting frustrated.

What would you tell a young person who is thinking about a career in writing?

I would tell that young person, above all, to enjoy the work and to understand that everything you do in your life contributes to your work. Now, I wouldn't advise anybody to live life as material for writing. At times I've lived my life under the sad delusion that suffering was good for my work. That gambit has never made me happier or more successful. Do what you like to do, read a lot and read what you like, and consider it a privilege to write. Also, take writing seriously and never be satisfied with the work you've accomplished. Be humble in your work. Even the most successful writers are an acquired taste. Finally, don't be jealous of other writers. They are your peers and your companions on a journey through the literary life.

Of course see your writing as a career skill, which is another reason to work constantly at honing that skill. Communicating well is a benefit in any profession, and skill as a writer is especially valuable in a digital world. Since writing books is rarely a viable livelihood, you'll likely need a career. If you choose teaching as that career, you'll find that communication in all forms is the most valuable skill you can possess. If I never wrote another poem, story, chapter of a novel, or essay, I would still, every day, write and speak publicly as part of my job.

Note: According to the U.S. Department of Education,[9] as many as 32 percent of college students transfer colleges during the course of their educational career. This is to say that the decision you initially make is not set in stone. Do your best to make a good choice, but remember that you can change your mind, your major, and even your campus. Many students do it and go on to have great experiences and earn great degrees.

Summary

This chapter covered all the aspects of college and post-secondary schooling that you'll want to consider as you move forward. Remember that finding the right fit is especially important as it increases the chances that you'll stay in school and earn your degree as well as have an amazing experience while you're at it.

In this chapter we discussed how to evaluate and compare your options in order to get the best education for the best deal. You also learned a little about scholarships and financial aid and how to write a unique personal statement that eloquently expresses your passions.

Use this chapter as a jumping-off point to dig deeper into your particular area of interest. Here are some tidbits of wisdom to leave you with.

- Take your SAT and ACT tests early in your junior year so you have time to take them again. Most universities automatically accept the highest scores.

- Make sure that the institution you plan to attend has an accredited program in your field of study. Some professions follow national accreditation policies while others are state-mandated and therefore differ across state lines. Do your research and understand the differences.
- Don't underestimate how important campus visits are especially in the pursuit of finding the right academic fit. Come prepared to ask questions not addressed on the school website or in the literature.
- Your personal statement is a very important piece of your application that can set you apart from others. Take the time and energy needed to make it unique and compelling.
- Don't assume you can't afford a school based on the "sticker price." Many schools offer great scholarships and aid to qualified students. It doesn't hurt to apply. This advice especially applies to minorities, veterans, and students with disabilities.
- Don't lose sight of the fact that it's important to pursue a career that you enjoy, are good at, and are passionate about! You'll be a happier person if you do so.

At this point, your career goals and aspirations should be gelling. At the least, you should have a plan for finding out more information. Remember to do the research about each university, school, or degree program that interests you before you reach out and especially before you visit. Faculty and staff find students who ask challenging questions much more impressive than those who ask questions that can be answered by spending ten minutes on the school website.

In chapter 4, we go into detail about the next steps: writing a résumé and cover letter, interviewing well, follow-up communications, and more. This is information you can use to secure internships, volunteer positions, and summer jobs, for example. It's not just for college grads. In fact, the sooner you can hone these communication skills, the better off you'll be in the professional world.

Writing Your Résumé and Interviewing

*W*ith each chapter of this book, we have narrowed the process from the broadest of strokes—what writers and authors do and what the difference is between the two, and what you can do with a writing-related degree, including jobs in publishing and business. In addition, we have covered how to plan your strategy and educational approach to making your dream job a reality.

In this chapter we will cover the steps involved in applying for jobs or schools: how to prepare an effective résumé and slam dunk an interview. Your résumé is your opportunity to summarize your experience, training, education, and goals and attract employers or school administrators. The goal of the résumé is to land the interview, and the goal of the interview is to land the job. Even if you do not have much work experience, you can still put together a résumé that expresses your interests and goals and the activities that illustrate your competence and interest.

Note: "Author" is of course not a job you apply for in the same way as you would apply for an editorial position. The process of getting a book published is different than applying for a more traditional job and entails preparing a proposal and reaching out to agents and editors who might want to see your work in print. There are many online resources that can guide you in the process of writing a book proposal and the elements you should include. (Every agent has a different submission policy so if you have an agent in mind, you want to find out what that is.) In general, a proposal will include a synopsis of the book; overview of the chapters; a sample chapter; details such as word count; market information such as competing or similar titles to indicate the size of audience for the book; and an author biography. In any case, for any profession you should have a strong résumé and know how to succeed in an interview.

As well as a résumé, you will be expected to write a cover letter that is basically your opportunity to reveal a little bit more about your passion, your motivation for a particular job or educational opportunity, and often whatever it is about you personally that will give your potential employer a sense of who you are and what drives you. And particularly because you are striving for a career in a very competitive and passion-based field, it's wise to ensure that your uniqueness, motivation, and commitment for working toward a meaningful goal—whatever it might be—comes through.

Giving the right impression is undoubtedly important but don't let that make you nervous. In a résumé, cover letter, or interview, you want to put forward your best but your genuine self. Dress professionally, proofread carefully (especially as you are applying for a job in the writing sphere!), and ensure you are being yourself. In this chapter, we will cover all of these important aspects of the job-hunting process, and by the end you will feel confident and ready to present yourself as a candidate for the job you really want.

Writing Your Résumé

Writing your first résumé can feel very challenging because you have likely not yet gained a lot of experience in a professional setting. But don't fret: employers understand that you are new to the workforce or to the particular career you are seeking. The right approach is never to exaggerate or invent experience or accomplishments but to present yourself as someone with a good work ethic and a genuine interest in that particular job or organization and to use what you can to present yourself authentically and honestly. And because you are pursuing a career in writing, having a portfolio of strong writing samples is a requirement. Your education speaks volumes but nothing makes a case for your qualifications like your own work.

THE MORE YOU READ, THE BETTER A WRITER YOU WILL BE

Marcia Santore.
Courtesy of Marcia Santore.

Marcia Santore is a freelance writer from New England. She specializes in nonfiction, working on projects for publishers, businesses, and nonprofit organizations as well as individual authors. She writes all kinds of things for all kinds of clients, including some of the books in this series. Her freelance business, Amalgamated Story, also provides developmental and copyediting for publishers and authors. She is a working artist and has illustrated and published several children's books. See her writing website at www.amalgamatedstory.com and her artwork at www.marciasantore.com.

What prompted you to pursue writing as a career and how have you used your writing experience to build a career?

Writing was always something I was good at, but I didn't think of pursuing it as a career at first because I was completely focused on being a painter. I did a lot of writing in high school—mostly poetry and short stories. There were two things that really influenced the way I write: One was my parents' dinner parties, which always involved people telling anecdotes around the table. That gave me a sense of how you tell a story to a listener. The other was writing letters, which I recommend highly. I got a lot of practice writing the stories of day-to-day life by writing letters to friends, grandparents, whomever. I kept a journal for a long time, which is basically writing letters to yourself. Like almost every other artist, I needed a day job to pay the bills. I worked at a series of jobs, mostly in academic institutions, starting in very lowly positions and slowly working my way up over the years. In each of those jobs, I found the opportunity to write and learn about how to fit the writing to meet the needs of particular projects. I have written all kinds of things: fundraising letters; grant proposals; short and long interviews; auction catalogs and product descriptions; bios of important people; annual reports; even assessment questions for text books. When I was editor of a university magazine, I got to use my writing skills to help people tell their stories. I love to hear people's stories so helping them tell them through the magazine was a joy. A university—both on campus and among the alumni—has so many people doing so many different things that there are always fascinating stories to be found. When I started my own freelance writing and editing business, I wanted to continue telling people's stories so those are the kinds of projects I seek most.

What is a typical day on the job for you?

I work from home, and I tend to write early in the day—partly because I'm just at my best in the morning and partly because my desk is under a window that faces west so there's a lot of sun in my eyes in the afternoon. That's generally a good hint that it's time to take a break. What I do next depends on what kind of projects I have going on. I check my messages to see who got back to me the night before and who needs what by when. There is always some time spent organizing and prioritizing (deadlines are great for prioritizing). I try to track how much time I'm spending working—both the paid work and the unpaid work—so I know what my hourly rate really is. If I have an interview scheduled, I'll phone the person and talk with them and then type up my notes into a more coherent narrative afterward. I might be doing research, collecting sources, quotes, and general information about a subject. I might be outlining or working on writing different sections of a piece. I work very intensely so I generally stop when my brain starts to hurt and then do other things like chores and errands in the afternoon.

What's the best part of your work in the writing field?

I like being in a state of flow, so when the writing is really going well, the hours fly by. I like the variety and learning new things—one day it might be researching a career I've barely heard of, another day it might be writing e-reader text for a fourth-grade math book. I also really like interviewing people. I live in a very small town and I work from home. As an introvert, that's a little too great for me. Interviews give me an opportunity to interact with many different people from many different places, at many different stages of their lives or careers, doing many different and fascinating things. It's all about the stories—hearing them, writing them, and sending them out there for others to enjoy.

What's the worst, or most challenging, part of your job in the writing field?

The most frustrating part of my job as a writer is the interviews! Not doing them, but arranging them. Sometimes I have to call a dozen potential subjects to get one person to agree to be interviewed. It's very time consuming and sort of emotionally exhausting. It's easier when they say no but often they just don't respond at all. Another challenge is keeping my inner writer from taking over when what I'm working on is not a writing job. When I'm working on an editing project, I can't just rewrite it. I have to rein that desire in and help the author come to the decision to rewrite it themselves. Another challenge is that freelance work is tidal—everything comes in at once, and everything goes away at once. So there are times when you have no clients and times when every client you ever worked for comes back plus three new ones. You have to learn to manage your time and your finances in this kind of work.

What is the most surprising thing about working in a writing-related profession?

I think something that comes as a surprise to many writers, especially early on, is that writing is very different from reading. All good writers start as readers. The more you read, and the better quality material you read, the better a writer you will be. But the process of reading (start at the beginning, move through the middle, come to the end) is not at all how writing works. A metaphor I sometimes use is that writing is more like Legos. You're building a structure from various elements, and it helps if you have an idea of what that structure is going to be. You need a strong foundation so it doesn't fall down. The way you put it together may well be by building different parts at different times—usually not in narrative order—and then combining them in the way that makes the most sense or the best story. This can involve taking sections apart and putting them back together differently, or in a different order, or throwing them out and building something else.

How do you combat writer's block? How do you stay motivated and avoid burnout?

Writer's block has never been a problem for me because I write nonfiction and I write for clients. I know what I need to communicate, how to research it, and how to put it together. My writing is creative but it's not my creative outlet, it's not my art form. I have been blocked as a painter, many times. It can feel awful, like you'll never work again, but what you learn over time is that creativity is also tidal. Sometimes the tide is out and you don't have any ideas. Sometimes the tide is in and you have more ideas than you can keep up with. The tricky part is remembering when the tide is out that it will come in again. So use that time constructively. For writers, that's when you get your manuscripts in order or dig out a short story you started but didn't have time to work on and see if you can polish it up. Research publishers and send some work out. Read! Read widely and see what sparks an idea. Don't watch yourself to see if ideas are coming—that's like trying to watch yourself fall asleep. And don't stop yourself from jotting down an idea because "you're blocked." Just relax, do other things, and let it come back when it's ready.

What would you tell a young person who is thinking about a career in writing?

Read. Read everything. Read online and on paper. Read quality—and don't limit your search for quality to what you already think it might be. Notice how other writers put sentences and paragraphs and books together. Read good books about writing (Stephen King's *On Writing* is a classic). Take writing classes, let people you trust read your early drafts, be open to comments and critiques but take them with a grain of salt. Finish things. It's easy to start a piece of writing but it's hard to finish it. If you can learn to finish a long-form piece, you're halfway there. Let your work marinate for a while, then come back and complete another draft. Finish that.

If you're writing nonfiction for a client, you might not have more than a day for that; if you're working on a novel with no deadline, you have all the time in the world so set yourself a day (month, year) when you'll come back to it.

If you want to be a freelance, nonfiction writer, you need to work up a portfolio of short and long projects. Starting at your day job is a great way to build a portfolio. If you don't have a writing job, find ways to write at your job. Write simply. Know grammar. Don't agonize over every sentence but listen to how they sound. Do your research to find publications that are looking for the kind of writing you want to do and submit some things—short articles and blog posts, for instance. Once you have a portfolio and you're ready to go freelance, remember that you're now a small business and need to keep track of things like taxes, marketing expenses, and health insurance. Finally, if someone wants you to sign a contract that makes the hair on the back of your neck stand up and they won't negotiate the terms, walk away.

There are some standard elements to an effective résumé that you should be sure to include. At the top should be your name, of course, as well as email address and other contact information. Always list your experience in chronological order, beginning with your current or most recent position—or whatever experience you want to share. If you are a recent graduate with little work experience, begin with your education. If you've been in the working world for a while, you can opt to list your education or any certification you have at the end. List anything you have published or any published work you may have edited.

> **Note:** You may need to customize your résumé for different purposes to ensure you are not filling it with information that does not directly relate to your qualifications for a particular job.

If this is your first résumé, be sure you highlight your education where you can—any courses you've taken be it in high school or through a community college or any other place that offers training related to your job target. Also highlight any hobbies or volunteer experience you have. But be concise: one page is usually appropriate, especially for your very first résumé.

> **Tip:** Before preparing your résumé, try to connect with a hiring professional—a human resources person or hiring manager—in a position or organization similar to the one you're interested in. They can give you advice on what employees look for and what information to highlight on your résumé as well as what types of interview questions you can expect.

As important as your résumé's content is the way you design and format it. You can find several samples online of résumés that you can be inspired by. At www.thebalancecareers.com,[1] for example, you can find many templates and design ideas. You want your résumé to be attractive to the eye and formatted in a way that makes the key points easy to spot and digest—according to some research, employers take an average of six seconds to review a résumé so you don't have a lot of time to get across your experience and value.

LinkingIn with Impact

As well as your paper or electronic résumé, creating a LinkedIn profile is a good way to highlight your experience and promote yourself as well as to network. Joining professional organizations or connecting with other people in your desired field are good ways to keep abreast of changes and trends and work opportunities.

The key elements of a LinkedIn profile are your photo, your headline, and your profile summary. These are the most revealing parts of the profile and the ones employers and connections will base their impression of you on.

The photo should be carefully chosen. Remember that LinkedIn is not Facebook or Instagram: it is not the place to share a photo of you acting too casually on vacation or at a party. According to Joshua Waldman, author of *Job Searching with Social Media for Dummies*,[2] the choice of photo should be taken seriously and be done right.

- Choose a photo in which you have a nice smile.
- Choose a photo that shows you in professional clothing.
- Ensure the background of the photo is pleasing to the eye. According to Waldman, some colors—like green and blue—convey a feeling of trust and stability.

- Remember it's not a mug shot. You can be creative with the angle of your photo rather than staring directly into the camera.
- Use your photo to convey some aspect of your personality.
- Focus on your face. Remember that visitors to your profile will see only a small thumbnail image so be sure your face takes up most of it.

WRITING AN OBJECTIVE

The objective section of your résumé is one of the most important as it is the first section a recruiter or hiring manager will read and therefore the first sense they will develop of you as a candidate. The objective should be brief but evocative. It should be focused and give a sense of you as a unique applicant—you don't want it to be generic or bland. It should show how creative you can be while keeping it professional. It's important to take your time and really refine your objective so you stand out and attract employers or clients.

Be sure you do your research on the job and organization or publisher you are applying to. Know exactly what kind of journalist, writer, editor, and so on the organization is looking for. Then you can better craft your objective to highlight the ways in which you uniquely match their needs.

"I love the independence of writing—just me and the keyboard, typing away. I love creating an online community around my words. I love the challenge of capturing the nuance of something ephemeral or complicated . . . When I am successful, I feel accomplished, productive, relevant, connected. The connection with readers is probably the best part of blogging. It is still surprising and humbling that strangers on the Internet take the time to read what I write and seem to care about what I have to say."—Sheila Quirke, freelance blogger and writer

Writing Your Cover Letter

As well as your résumé, most employers will ask you to submit a cover letter. This is a one-page letter in which you express your motivation, why you are interested in the organization or position, and what skills you possess that make you the right fit for the position.

Here are some tips for writing an effective cover letter.

- As always, proofread your text carefully before submitting it. This is important in any job field but particularly if you are submitting yourself as a candidate for a job in writing or editing.
- Be sure you have a letter that is focused on a specific job. Do not make it too general or one-size-fits-all. Your personality and uniqueness should come through or the recruiter or hiring manager will move on to the next application. Again, particularly for a career in journalism or media, your writing style and "voice" will be important in helping you stand out from the competition.
- Summarize why you are right for the position. Keep it relevant and specific to what the particular publication or organization is looking for in a candidate and employee.
- Keep your letter to one page whenever possible.
- Introduce yourself in a way that makes the reader want to know more about you and encourages them to review your résumé.
- Be specific about the job you are applying for. Mention the title and be sure it is correct.
- Try to find the name of the person who will receive your letter rather than making the salutation non-specific (e.g., "To whom it may concern").
- Be sure you include your contact details.
- End with a "call to action"—a request for an interview, for example.

Interviewing Skills

With your sparkling résumé, LinkedIn profile, and writing samples, you are bound to be called in for an interview. This is an important stage to reach: you will have already gone through several filters—your potential employer has gotten a quick look at your experience and has reviewed your LinkedIn profile and has made the decision to learn more about you in person.

> "If you don't have time to read, you don't have the time (or the tools) to write. Simple as that."—Stephen King (1947), American author of horror, supernatural fiction, suspense, crime, science-fiction, and fantasy novels

Be it in person or via video call, a job interview can be stressful. You can help calm your nerves and feel more confident if you prepare ahead by thinking about answers to questions you may be asked. *Inside Creative House/iStock/Getty Images.*

There's no way to know ahead of time exactly what to expect in an interview, but there are many ways to prepare yourself. You can start by learning more about the person who will be interviewing you. In the same way recruiters and employers can learn about you online, you can do the same. You can see if you have any education or work experience in common or any contacts you both know. It's perfectly acceptable and even considered proactive to research the person with whom you'll be interviewing, such as on LinkedIn.

Preparing yourself for the types of questions you will be asked to ensure you offer thoughtful and meaningful responses is vital to interview success.

Note: Depending on the position for which you are applying, you may be asked to do an editing or writing test as part of the interview process. This can entail editing a piece of writing according to house style as well as the standard rules of grammar, spelling, and punctuation; or writing a short text (an article or blog post, for example) in a set amount of time. There's no real way to prepare for this except to know to expect it. The test will be designed to ensure you can perform at the quality level necessary and in a timely manner, under pressure. Just take a deep breath and do your best.

BEWARE WHAT YOU SHARE ON SOCIAL MEDIA

Most of us engage in social media. And for writers and journalists, it's pretty much a necessity for building an audience and having a platform to share your writing skills and point of view and to give others a sense of what news and stories you find most important.

Sites such as Facebook, Twitter, and Instagram provide us with a platform for sharing photos and memories, opinions, and life events, revealing everything from our political stance to our sense of humor. It's a great way to connect with people around the world, but once you post something, it's accessible to anyone—including potential employers—unless you take mindful precautions.

Your posts may be public, which means you may be making the wrong impression without realizing it. More and more, people are using search engines like Google to get a sense of potential employers, colleagues, or employees, and the impression you make online can have a strong impact on how you are perceived. Approximately 70 percent of employers[3] search for information on candidates on social media sites.

Glassdoor.com[4] offers the following tips on how to keep your social media activity from sabotaging your career success.

1. Check your privacy settings. Ensure that your photos and posts are only accessible to the friends or contacts you want to see them. In the photos that are available to the public you want to come across as professional and reliable.
2. Rather than avoiding social media while searching for a job, use it to your advantage. Especially as a journalist or media job applicant, it's to your advantage to have an online presence (as long as it's a flattering one). Give future employees a sense of your professional interest by liking pages or joining professional organizations related to your career goals.
3. Grammar counts. Be attentive to the quality of writing of all your posts and comments.
4. Be consistent. With each social media outlet, there is a different focus and tone to what you are communicating. LinkedIn is very professional while Facebook is far more social and relaxed. It's okay to adopt a different tone on various social media sites but be sure you aren't blatantly contradicting yourself.
5. Choose your username carefully. Remember, social media may be the first impression anyone has of you in the professional realm.

Consider your answers carefully and be prepared to support them with examples and anecdotes.

Here are some questions you should be prepared to be asked. It's a good idea to consider your answers carefully without memorizing what you mean to say (as that can throw you off and will be obvious to the interviewer). Think carefully about your responses and be prepared to deliver them in a natural manner.

- Why did you decide to enter this field? What drives your passion for working in the writing and publishing industry?
- What is your educational background? What credentials did you earn?
- What publishing experience do you have as an editor or writer? What are some of your favorite books or publications?
- Are you a regular reader/listener/viewer of our work and if so, what do you like about it ? What might you want to make different?
- Are you a team player? Describe your usual role in a team-centered work environment. Do you easily assume a leadership role?

DRESSING APPROPRIATELY

How you dress for a job interview is very important to the impression you want to make. Remember that the interview, no matter what the actual environment in which you'd be working, is your chance to present your most professional self. Although you will not likely ever wear a suit to work, for the interview it's the most professional choice.

> **Tip:** A suit may no longer be an absolute requirement in many job interviews, but avoid looking too casual as it will give the impression you are not that interested in the job or the organization.

WHAT EMPLOYERS EXPECT

Hiring managers and human resource professionals will also have certain expectations of you at an interview. The main thing is preparation: it cannot be overstated that you should arrive to an interview appropriately dressed, on time, unhurried, and ready to answer—and ask—questions.

TO SHAKE OR NOT TO SHAKE?

A handshake is a traditional form of greeting especially in business. When you arrive for a job interview—or just meet someone new—a good, firm handshake shows that you are a person to be taken seriously.

But shaking hands is not done in every culture, and even in North America, the norm of shaking hands has changed. During the COVID–19 crisis, people have stopped shaking hands in order to avoid spreading germs. As things get back to normal, some people will want to resume shaking hands and some people won't. This means that when you arrive for a job interview, the best thing is to follow the lead of the person you're meeting. A respectful head nod is just fine.

Shaking hands in the twenty-first century is something to think about. *PeopleImages/iStock/ Getty Images.*

For any job interview, the main things employers will look for are that you

- have a thorough understanding of the organization and the job for which you are applying.
- are prepared to answer questions about yourself and your relevant experience.

- are poised and likeable but still professional. They will be looking for a sense of what it would be like to work with you on a daily basis and how your presence would fit in the culture of the business.
- stay engaged. Listen carefully to what is being asked and offer thoughtful but concise answers. Don't blurt out answers you've memorized but really focus on what is being asked.
- are prepared to ask your own questions. It shows how much you understand the flow of an organization or workplace and how you will contribute to it. Here are some questions you can ask:

  ○ What created the need to fill this position? Is it a new position or has someone left the organization?
  ○ Where does this position fit in the overall hierarchy of the organization?
  ○ What are the key skills required to succeed in this job?
  ○ What challenges might I expect to face within the first six months on the job?
  ○ How does this position relate to the achievement of the company's (or department's, or boss's) goals?
  ○ How would you describe this organization's culture?

HAVE A THICK SKIN AND KEEP ON WRITING

Annie L. Scholl.
Courtesy of Annie L. Scholl.

Annie L. Scholl got her bachelor's in journalism and mass communication from the University of Iowa in 1985. She worked as a newspaper reporter for about fifteen years, the bulk of that time for the *Cedar Rapids Gazette* in her hometown. She worked in marketing for about ten years before starting Annie Scholl Creative in 2010. Annie was a full-time freelance writer for another ten years before taking a full-time position as a senior content writer for a higher education marketing firm. Annie, who is at work on a memoir, blogs at www.anniescholl.com and contributes to

Huffington Post as a guest writer. She also writes regularly for *Unity Magazine*, *Daily Word*, and Sunlight Press. Her work has been published by Brevity and Past Ten as well as other online outlets. She lives in North Carolina with her wife Michelle and their two dogs and three cats.

Why did you choose to become a writer?

In fourth grade I wrote a story sparked by an experience with my two little sisters. I asked my art teacher if she would do the illustrations for it. She did. I remember stapling an orange construction paper cover on it. Maybe it all started there.

When I graduated from high school, my plan was to become an English teacher like my beloved teacher Carolyn Taylor. I went to the University of Northern Iowa, what was known then as a teachers college, and I was miserable. I decided to transfer to the University of Iowa because it was closer to home. When I was going through the course catalog I found the BA in journalism and mass communication. I knew instantly that's what I wanted to do. I earned my degree in four years, graduated, and went right to work for a small daily in northwest Iowa. I was a general assignment reporter there and quickly learned hard news reporting wasn't for me. I worked as a feature writer at the *Green Bay Press-Gazette* for about a year before moving back to my hometown to take a job at the *Cedar Rapids Gazette*. I left daily newspaper writing in December 2000. For the past twenty years I've primarily worked as a higher education marketing writer but I also still freelance and am at work on a memoir.

What is a typical day like for you?

I meditate every morning. Any personal writing—work on my memoir, a blog post— I'll do in the morning because it's my best time to write. Most days my wife and I walk our dogs and then have coffee together on our back deck. I then dive into my work as a senior content writer. Most of my days are spent writing web pages, landing pages, social media ads, and messaging and personnel documents. I've been taking a writing class and working one-on-one with my teacher to finish my memoir so a couple evenings a week are dedicated to that.

What's the best part of your job?

Telling stories and making connections. In August 2020, a devastating derecho (a hurricane-like storm) hit my beloved Iowa. While my family and friends were dealing with no power and the destruction of their homes and properties, I was in North Carolina a thousand miles away feeling helpless. The only way I could think of to help was to write, to bring attention to a story the national media had largely ignored. I wrote a piece that was published on Huffington Post. I also wrote a blog for my personal website. Both were widely read and shared. Yes, plenty of Internet trolls had hateful things to say, but I heard from dozens who thanked me for writing, who said I expressed what they were feeling. Knowing that something I wrote helped someone or moved someone—to tears, laughter, or action—is why I love being a writer. Even in my work as a marketing writer, I'm trying to make an emotional connection with the reader. I also love seeing my words come to life in a webpage design or a magazine article. I still get a kick out of that after thirty-five years.

What's the worst or most challenging part of your job?

Being misunderstood. You write something and you put it out in the world and you have no control over how it's received or perceived. You know what your intention was when you wrote it but people can only read through their own lens. My skin is mighty thick after three and a half decades as a writer, but the criticism can still sting. I also battle crippling self-doubt at times where I just want to hang it up as a writer. That's not true in my marketing work—I feel very confident in that arena—but it does come into play in my personal writing. I try and shift out of that place of fear, that place of ego, and instead focus on being of service—of writing something that someone, somewhere needs to hear.

What's the most surprising thing about your job?

Sometimes I'm amazed at what comes up when I write. I'll read back over something and think, wow, where did that come from? It's not of my conscious creation. When I allow the writing to come from my heart versus my head, that's when I do my best work. In my work as a marketing writer, what surprises me is how much I still have to learn. Marketing is continually evolving, particularly writing for the Web. I've been doing this work since 2002 and I'm still learning. That's what I love about it, too.

What kinds of qualities do you think one needs to be successful at this job?

Curiosity. Compassion. Perseverance. A thick skin. An open heart. A willingness to put yourself out there and be vulnerable. A willingness to take what comes in the form of criticism without taking it personally or internalizing it. As a marketing writer, you have to be curious and know how to ask questions and listen to answers so that you can emotionally connect with consumers. With that said, I couldn't market something I didn't believe in so writing for higher ed is an ideal fit for me. I like helping people find the right college or university where they can learn what they need to learn to bring their dreams to life.

How do you combat stress and burnout?

I definitely felt burned out when I was writing daily for a newspaper. I was primarily writing personality profiles, and while I loved interviewing people and sharing their stories, cranking out a half-dozen or more each week made me feel like a factory worker. I do get stressed with my marketing work—I have a lot on my plate and constant deadlines to meet—but the truth is I do my best work under pressure. I wish I didn't but I do. When it all gets too much, I just step away, have a good cry, talk with my wife or one of my sisters, drink wine, eat chocolate, get a massage, schedule therapy. Then I get back to it. Even when I want to quit, I know I can't. I'm a writer. It's how I process what's happening in my life and in the world.

What would you tell a young person who is thinking about a career in writing?

When I was in journalism school, I had to write a piece and then share it with my source. He tore it apart and I was devastated. I went crying to my professor and he told me if I couldn't handle criticism, I best pick a different career. I knew this was mine to do so I wasn't going to quit—despite being a sensitive person. You do have to have a thick skin as a writer. You are going to be misunderstood. You are going to be criticized. Editors are going to critique your work. You have to be willing to write and rewrite. But when you write something and it lands on somebody, when what you wrote made them laugh or cry—or when they say, "Thank you for putting words to what I've been feeling," well, it really doesn't get any better.

If you want to write, write. Don't give in to the negative voices, particularly your own. Be willing to work at your craft. Read and write. Take classes and workshops. Keep going.

Summary

Congratulations on working through the book! You should now have a strong idea of your career goals within the writing field and how to realize them. In this chapter, we covered how to present yourself as the right candidate to a potential employer—and these strategies are also relevant if you are applying to a college or another form of training.

Here are some tips to sum it up.

- Your résumé should be concise and focused on relevant aspects of your work experience or education. Although you can include some personal hobbies or details, they should be related to the job and your qualifications for it.

- Take your time with all your professional documents—your résumé, your cover letter, your LinkedIn profile—and be sure to proofread very carefully to avoid embarrassing and sloppy mistakes.
- Prepare yourself for an interview by anticipating the types of questions you will be asked and coming up with professional and meaningful responses.
- Equally, prepare questions to ask your potential employer at the interview. This will show you have a good understanding and interest in the organization and what role you would have in it.
- Always follow up an interview with a letter or an email. An email is the fastest way to express your gratitude for the interviewer's time and restate your interest in the position.
- Dress appropriately for the interview and pay extra attention to tidiness and hygiene.
- Be wary of what you share on social media sites while job searching. Most employers research candidates online, and what you have shared will influence their idea of who you are and what it would be like to work with you.

You've chosen to pursue a career in a competitive, challenging, but also broad and exciting field. I wish you great success with your future.

Notes

Introduction

1. Merriam-Webster, "author," www.merriam-webster.com/dictionary/author; Merriam-Webster, "writer," www.merriam-webster.com/dictionary/writer.

2. /www.bls.gov/ooh/media-and-communication/writers-and-authors.htm.

Chapter 1

1. Neil Gutkind, "What Is Creative Nonfiction?" creativenonfiction.org, www.creativenonfiction.org/online-reading/what-creative-nonfiction.

2. Nick Douglas, "Why You Should Write for Free," Lifehacker, https://lifehacker.com/why-you-should-write-for-free-1823900900.

3. John Scalzi, "No, In Fact, You Should Not Write For Free," scalzi.com, https://whatever.scalzi.com/2018/03/20/no-in-fact-you-should-not-write-for-free.

4. Bureau of Labor Statistics, "Agents and Business Managers of Artists, Performers, and Athletes," www.bls.gov/oes/current/oes131011.htm.

5. Bureau of Labor Statistics, "Editor," www.bls.gov/ooh/media-and-communication/editors.htm.

6. Concepción de León, "Does It Pay to Be a Writer?" *New York Times*, January 5, 2019, www.nytimes.com/2019/01/05/books/authors-pay-writer.html.

7. Jim Milliot and Rachel Deahl, "What's the Matter with Fiction Sales?" *Publishers Weekly*, October 26, 2018, www.publishersweekly.com/pw/by-topic/industry-news/publisher-news/article/78446-what-s-the-matter-with-fiction-sales.html.

8. Colin Ainsworth, "Book Sales Are Soaring—And Not Just the Digital Kind," Mental Floss, www.mentalfloss.com/article/570930/book-sales-are-soaring.

9. U.S. Bureau of Labor Statistics, "Reporters, Correspondents, and Broadcast News Analysts," www.bls.gov/ooh/media-and-communication/reporters-correspondents-and-broadcast-news-analysts.htm#tab-3.

10. Jessica Klein, "35% of the U.S. Workforce Is Now Freelancing—10 Million More Than 5 Years Ago," Fast Company, www.fastcompany.com/90411808/35-of-the -u-s-workforce-is-now-freelancing-10-million-more-than-5-years-ago.

11. Angelica Hartgers, "Detailed Author Salary Report: How Much Do Authors Make?" selfpublishing.com, https://selfpublishing.com/author-salary/#6.

Chapter 2

1. www.allthetests.com, "Are You a Writer at Heart?" www.allthetests.com/ quiz28/quiz/1292437291/Are-You-a-Writer-at-Heart.

2. Sheryl Burgstahler, Sara Lopez, and Scott Bellman, "Preparing for a Career: An Online Tutorial," DO-IT, www.washington.edu/doit/preparing-career-online-tutorial.

Chapter 3

1. National Center for Education Statistics, "Fast Facts: Graduation Rates," https://nces.ed.gov/fastfacts/display.asp?id=40.

2. U.S. Department of Education, "Focusing Higher Education on Student Success," www.ed.gov/news/press-releases/fact-sheet-focusing-higher-education-stu dent-success.

3. National Center for Education Statistics, "Table 502.30. Median Annual Earnings of Full-Time Year-Round Workers 25 to 34 Years Old and Full-Time Year-Round Workers as a Percentage of the Labor Force, by Sex, Race/Ethnicity, and Educational Attainment: Selected Years, 1995 through 2013," https://nces.ed.gov/programs/digest/ d14/tables/dt14_502.30.asp; U.S. Bureau of Labor Statistics, "Current Population Survey," www.bls.gov/cps/cpsaat07.htm.

4. Dr. Steven R. Antonoff, U.S. News & World Report, "College Personality Quiz," July 31, 2018, www.usnews.com/education/best-colleges/right-school/choices/articles/ college-personality-quiz.

5. Alex Gailey, "Taking a Gap Year During Coronavirus? Here's How to Make the Most of It," Next Advisor, https://time.com/nextadvisor/in-the-news/gap-year-coron avirus/.

6. Koppelman Group, "The Best Undergraduate Creative Writing Programs," www.koppelmangroup.com/blog/2017/11/5/the-best-undergraduate-creative-writ ing-programs.

7. www.niche.com, "2021 Best Colleges for English in America," www.niche .com/colleges/search/best-colleges-for-english/.

8. Farran Powell and Emma Kerr, "See the Average College Tuition in 2020– 2021," *U.S. News & World Report*, September 14, 2020, www.usnews.com/education/ best-colleges/paying-for-college/articles/paying-for-college-infographic.

9. National Center for Education Statistics, "Six-Year Attainment, Persistence, Transfer, Retention, and Withdrawal Rates of Students Who Began Postsecondary Education in 2003–04," https://nces.ed.gov/pubs2011/2011152.pdf.

Chapter 4

1. Alison Doyle, "Student Résumé Examples, Templates, and Writing Tips," The Balance Careers, www.thebalancecareers.com/student-resume-examples-and-tem plates-2063555.

2. Joshua Waldman, *Job Searching with Social Media for Dummies* (Hoboken, NJ: Wiley & Sons, 2013).

3. SecurityMagazine.com, "70 Percent of Employers Check Candidates' Social Media Profiles," www.securitymagazine.com/articles/89441-percent-of-employers -check-candidates-social-media-profiles.

4. Alice A. M. Underwood, "9 Things to Avoid on Social Media While Looking for a New Job," Glassdoor, www.glassdoor.com/blog/things-to-avoid-on-social-media -job-search.

Glossary

author: a person who writes a piece of published, original work

bachelor's degree: a four-year degree awarded by a college or university

blogger: a person who produces online content for a blog, usually from their own perspective and based on a particular subject matter

burnout: a feeling of physical and emotional exhaustion caused by overwork

campus: the location of a school, college, or university

career assessment test: a test that asks questions particularly geared to identify skills and interests to help inform the test taker on what type of career would suit them

colleagues: the people with whom one works

community college: a two-year college that awards associate degrees

cover letter: a letter that usually accompanies a résumé and allows a candidate applying to a job or a school or internship an opportunity to describe their motivation and qualifications

creative nonfiction: a piece of writing that is based on real people and events but is written in a literary style

editor: a person whose job it is to work with an author to offer feedback and help refine and polish a piece of work so that it is ready for publication

educational background: the degrees a person has earned and schools attended

fiction: a style of writing in which the story, characters, and plot are the invention of the writer

financial aid: various means of receiving financial support for the purpose of attending school. This can be a grant or scholarship, for example.

freelancer: a person who owns their own business through which they provide services to a variety of clients

gap year: a year between high school and higher education or employment during which a person can explore their passions and interests, often while traveling

General Education Development (GED) degree: an earned degree that is equivalent to a high school diploma

industry: the people and activities involved in one type of business, such as the business of publishing

internship: a work experience opportunity that lasts for a set period of time and can be paid or unpaid

in-state school: a non-private college in the state in which the student is a resident. In-state schools offer lower tuitions to state residents.

interpersonal skills: the ability to communicate and interact with other people in an effective manner

interviewing: a part of the job-seeking process in which the candidate meets with a potential employer, usually face to face, in order to discuss their work experience and education and seek information about the job

job market: a market in which employers search for employees and employees search for jobs

literary agent: a person whose job it is to represent an author and his or her work in order to sell the work to a publisher. An agent also negotiates the contract between an author and publisher.

major: the subject or course of study in which a person chooses to earn their degree

master's degree: a degree that is sought by those who have already earned a bachelor's degree in order to further their education

master's of fine arts degree: a master's degree that is particularly focused on a creative rather than research-based subject, such as creative writing

networking: the process of building, strengthening, and maintaining professional relationships as a way to further career goals

out-of-state school: a non-private college that exists in a state other than that in which the student is a resident. These schools have higher tuitions for non-state residents.

portfolio: a collection of work, such as writing, that represents the talents and abilities of the person who created it

résumé: a document, usually one page, that outlines a person's professional experience and education and that is designed to give potential employers a sense of the candidate's qualifications

social media: websites and applications that enable users to create and share content online for networking and social-sharing purposes. Examples include Facebook and Instagram.

tuition: the money a student pays for his or her education

work culture: a concept that defines the beliefs, philosophy, thought processes, and attitudes of employees in a particular organization

writer: someone who writes for a living but focuses on work such as copywriting, technical writing, or advertising

Further Resources

The following websites, magazines, blogs, and podcasts can help you further investigate and educate yourself on writer- and author-related topics, all of which will help you as you take the next steps in your career now and throughout your professional life.

Publications and Websites

Editor and Publisher—A print and online publication dedicated to the publishing and editing industry (www.editorandpublisher.com).

Blogger Magazine—An online magazine that publishes blogs on a variety of topics including how to market yourself as a blogger. Offers inspiration for bloggers (http://bloggermagazine.net).

Poets and Writers—A nonprofit organization, including a website and print magazine, that has been serving creative writers since 1970 and offering programs for writers as well as hosting writing competitions and other benefits (www.pw.org).

The Creative Independent, "How to Write a Book Proposal"—An illustrated and detailed online guide to preparing a book proposal to catch the eye of agents and editors (https://thecreativeindependent.com/guides/how-to-write-a-book-proposal/).

Blogs

Writing Forward—A great source of tips and ideas to keep your creative juices flowing, from grammar tips to writing prompts (www.writingforward.com).

Terribleminds—Novelist Chuck Wendig's blog is an excellent example of how to build an online platform as an author. It provides a wealth of tips on fiction writing (www.terribleminds.com/ramble/blog).

Creative Writing News—A site focusing on helping those who want to earn money from their writing. It provides information on writing competitions, literary events, and scholarships and prizes (www.creativewritingnews.com).

Podcasts

Writing Excuses—An educational podcast for writers, by writers, with the goal to help listeners improve as writers. With the tagline "Fifteen minutes long because you're in a hurry and we're not that smart," the very smart hosts offer a new episode of 15–25 minutes each Sunday (www. writing excuses.com).

A Way with Words—An intelligent, entertaining, and always enlightening podcast and radio show about language as understood via family, history, and culture. Discover the origin of words such as "dogberg" and "asthenosphere" (www.waywordradio.org).

The Creative Writer's Toolbelt—A podcast offering a plethora of advice and encouragement to creative writers with each episode focusing on a specific technique of the writing craft. Some episodes feature interviews with guest authors (https://ajc-cwt-001.podomatic.com).

The Guardian Books Podcast—On this podcast listeners are treated to a weekly episode covering all things books including in-depth interviews with writers from around the world and discussions of books and publishing (www.theguardian.com/books/series/books).

Bibliography

Ainsworth, Colin. "Book Sales Are Soaring—And Not Just the Digital Kind." *Mental Floss*. (January 17, 2019.) www.mentalfloss.com/article/570930/book-sales-are-soaring.

Allthetests.com. "Are You a Writer at Heart?" developed on December 15, 2010. www.allthetests.com/quiz28/quiz/1292437291/Are-You-a-Writer-at-Heart.

Antonoff, Dr. Steven R. "College Personality Quiz." *U.S. News & World Report*. July 31, 2018. www.usnews.com/education/best-colleges/right-school/choices/articles/college-personality-quiz.

Cain, Elna. "How to Become a Writer and Make a Living in 2020 (Complete Guide)." *Elna Cain*. https://elnacain.com/blog/become-a-writer.

Capuzzi Simon, Cecilia. "Why Writers Love to Hate the M.F.A." *New York Times*, April 9, 2015. www.nytimes.com/2015/04/12/education/edlife/12edl-12mfa.html?auth=login-email&login=email&login=email&auth=login-email.

de León, Concepción. "Does It Pay to Be a Writer?" *New York Times*, January 5, 2019. www.nytimes.com/2019/01/05/books/authors-pay-writer.html.

Douglas, Nick. "Why You Should Write for Free." *LifeHacker*. March 20, 2018. https://lifehacker.com/why-you-should-write-for-free-1823900900.

Gailey, Alex. "Taking a Gap Year During Coronavirus? Here's How to Make the Most of It." *Next Advisor*. March 10, 2021. https://time.com/nextadvisor/in-the-news/gap-year-coronavirus/.

Gutkind, Neil. "What Is Creative Nonfiction?" *Creative Nonfiction*. www.creativenonfiction.org/online-reading/what-creative-nonfiction.

Hartgers, Angelica. "Detailed Author Salary Report: How Much Do Authors Make?" *Self-Publishing School*. February 4, 2020. https://selfpublishing.com/author-salary/#6.

Klein, Jessica. "35% of the U.S. Workforce Is Now Freelancing—10 Million More Than 5 Years Ago." *Fast Company*. October 3, 2019. www.fastcompany.com/90411808/35-of-the-u-s-workforce-is-now-freelancing-10-million-more-than-5-years-ago.

Klems, Brian K. "The 8 Elements of a Nonfiction Book Proposal." *Writer's Digest*, June 28, 2012. www.writersdigest.com/whats-new/the-8-essential -elements-of-a-nonfiction-book-proposal.

Koppelman Group. "The Best Undergraduate Creative Writing Programs." November 5, 2017. www.koppelmangroup.com/blog/2017/11/5/ the-best-undergraduate-creative-writing-programs.

Merriam-Webster. "Author." www.merriam-webster.com/dictionary/author.

———. "Writer." www.merriam-webster.com/dictionary/writer.

Milliot, Jim and Rachel Deahl. "What's the Matter with Fiction Sales?" *Publishers Weekly*, October 26, 2018.

Niche.com. "2021 Best Colleges for English in America." www.niche.com/ colleges/search/best-colleges-for-english.

Ogle, Sean. "The Exact 10 Steps You Need to Learn to Be a Writer." *Location Rebel*. April 11, 2018. www.locationrebel.com/how-to-become-a-writer.

Powell, Farran and Emma Kerr. "See the Average College Tuition in 2020– 2021." *U.S. News & World Report*, September 14, 2020. www.usnews.com/ education/best-colleges/paying-for-college/articles/paying-for-college-info graphic.

Scalzi, John. "No, in Fact, You Should Not Write for Free." *Whatever: Early Days of a Better Nation*. March 20, 2018. https://whatever.scalzi .com/2018/03/20/no-in-fact-you-should-not-write-for-free.

SecurityMagazine.com. "70 Percent of Employers Check Candidates' Social Media Profiles." September 23, 2018. www.securitymagazine.com/arti cles/89441-percent-of-employers-check-candidates-social-media-profiles.

U.S. Bureau of Labor Statistics. "Writers and Authors." www.bls.gov/ooh/ media-and-communication/writers-and-authors.htm.

———. "Agents and Business Managers of Artists, Performers, and Athletes." www.bls.gov/oes/current/oes131011.htm.

———. "Editor." www.bls.gov/ooh/media-and-communication/editors.htm.

About the Author

Tracy Brown Hamiton is a writer, editor, and journalist based in the Netherlands. She has written several books on topics ranging from careers to media and economics to pop culture. She lives with her husband and three children.

Lightning Source UK Ltd.
Milton Keynes UK
UKHW021446240822
407769UK00011B/243